ONE STEP AT A TIME

The Wilberforce Way

Paul Amess

Kingston House Publishing

CONTENTS

The Wilberforce Way

Introduction

In my time, I've walked many of the country's long-distance paths, all of which have usually involved blisters as well as a long journey just to get to the start, so I was thrilled to bits when I found out about the Wilberforce Way, a delightful little amble that is right on my own doorstep, with the odd pub along the way. As for the blisters, I'd just have to hope for the best.

My good friend Rob is coming along for the ride too, and he will also be the entertainment, probably. He tends to say strange and funny things, as do I, and along the way, we hope to be learning about the people and the places, and let's just say we tend to focus on the more obscure stuff that they never teach you in school.

This isn't actually a guidebook, either. If you

try to use this as one, consider yourself warned. You'll either wake up in a police cell one morning with something of a hangover, or your family will report you missing after a few days, never to see you again. Rob and I are both a bit stupid, you see, but we are fun, so if that sounds like you, please come with us and find out all about what the Wilberforce Way has to offer.

As for my being stupid, I've known this since I was at school, and since one incident in particular, which was an awkward moment when my entire maths class was discussing whether the answer to a problem was 142 or 144, and my answer was negative 936. So we really don't care if you're laughing with us or at us, so long as you're laughing. And we usually try to set an example to others, though to be honest, it is usually a bad example, it has to be said.

Silly things tend to happen, you see. For instance, I popped into the supermarket last night to get some lunch for the first day of this walk. The lady in front of me was perhaps expecting the apocalypse and seemed to have done approximately three months' worth of shopping, and it took an age for it all to be scanned and put back in her trolley.

The guy on the till said the bill came to one hundred and forty-seven pounds and ten pence, and then he jokingly asked the lady's son if all this food was for him. After the boy nodded, the man then asked him if it all goes in his mouth and fills up his hollow legs, pointing at the boy's legs as he did so. As young and innocent children tend to do, the boy then said something really funny and said that yes, it did go in there, and then it comes out here and pointed at his backside. On a positive note, this did pass the time in the queue.

And going on this walk will at least keep me from being under my wife's feet for a few days. Don't get me wrong, we love each other very much. It's just that lately, I've been home a bit more than usual as I recently lost my job due to a misunderstanding. My boss told me not to dress for the job I had, but to dress for the job I wanted. But when I turned up at the office the next day dressed as a ghostbuster, the weasel said I was fired.

We've been married for 20 years and have never once thought about divorce. Murder, yes. But divorce, no. She can be so funny sometimes. She thinks that her long silences or *'I won't talk to you'* attitude is actually a punishment, bless her.

I try to pass on some of my wisdom to my kids, too, just so they are prepared when they finally meet the one of their dreams and can thus handle the relationship with all the eloquence of a lobster, just like their dad. For instance, I have taught them that in any relationship, the wife always has the last word in any argument. After that last word, anything the husband says should actually be classed as the beginning of a new argument.

Furthermore, a scientific study has proven that women with extra weight usually live longer than men who point it out. I teach them other stuff, too, because I'm awesome. For instance, my son wanted to know what it's like to be married, so I told him to leave me alone, and when he did, I asked him why he was ignoring me.

My advice is not just restricted to marriage, either, as I want them to do well in all aspects of life, including the world of work, so I've taught them handy snippets such as the fact that the first five days after the weekend are the toughest, and lastly, and this is a good one, when you hear the doorbell, always answer with your jacket in your hand. Depending on who's there, you see, you can either say you've only just come in or you're just about to leave. You're welcome.

Anyway, getting back to the walk that is the Wilberforce Way, it really is a good one. Running from the beautiful city of York, this sixty-mile wander leads you through delightful meadows and plains, weaves through some beautiful and interesting Yorkshire villages, and skirts the hills of the Yorkshire Wolds before bringing you down into the smart little market town of Beverley and finishing in the amazing city of Kingston-Upon-Hull.

The name relates to William Wilberforce, who is linked to many places along the way, and who fought hard throughout his lifetime to abolish slavery, a concept he described as *the odious traffic in human flesh*. Ironically, some of the family fortune that Wilberforce inherited came from profits made from refining sugar from the West Indies, an industry which relied greatly on slavery itself.

That Wilberforce ultimately succeeded in his goal of outlawing slavery is in itself quite an accomplishment. Slavery was so much a part of the global economy in the late 1700s that nobody could imagine a world without slaves. Add to that the fact that more than a few people were making vast sums of money from slavery, and we can at least get a picture of the opposition he faced. But what this resulted in was a prize that was beyond value, and that prize was the moral high ground, which, let's face it, was not normal territory for the British Empire at the time. You see, Britain became the first major world power to make the moral choice to deliberately end its own incredibly profitable slave trade and then work towards the abolition of slavery worldwide. Once again, world, you're welcome.

And before we go on, I have to mention that when we talk of the abolition of slavery, we are only talking of that in a legal sense. Slavery has never actually been abolished as such, and as long as people exist, it never will be. It has merely been made illegal, and then only sort of.

In fact, there are more people enslaved in the world right now than at any point in history, despite it being illegal in every single country in the world, as reported by *The New York Times* anyway. The truth is much less clear, however. According to a different article that appeared in *The Independent* in 2020, there are 94 countries dotted around the globe where slavery is not a crime, meaning that a person cannot even be prosecuted for enslaving another human being, which is absolute madness.

And while it is true that actual legal ownership of people has indeed been abolished in all countries of the world, this is not at all the same as saying that slavery has been abolished. In fact, 180 states, or in laymen's terms, 93 per cent of the world's countries, appear not to have enacted legislative provisions criminalising servitude, which is not just alarming, but is actually criminal. However, we should not let this reality undermine what William Wilberforce did for the emancipation of enslaved peoples worldwide, for without him, the world would be a much darker place than it is now, and let's be honest, it isn't all that great anyway.

As for Wilberforce, he was born in 1759 in Hull, went to school in Pocklington, and then moved on to university in Cambridge, though he actually spent most of his time there playing cards and getting incredibly drunk with his friends. However, he eventually settled down, becoming a Member of Parliament in 1780, initially representing Hull and later the whole of Yorkshire. Using much of his time in office to push for the abolition of slavery, something which moved closer in 1807 when the Slave Trade Act was eventually passed by parliament, he became the de facto leader of the abolitionist movement for much of his life. Incidentally, while Wilberforce's name is forever linked to the abolition of the slave trade, what is less well known is that he was also a founding member of the RSPCA, *The Royal Society for the Prevention of Cruelty to Animals*, which campaigned vigorously for laws to protect animals.

While many thought that the 1807 Act would end the slave trade once and for all, it did not actually make slavery illegal, it merely made the trade in slaves illegal. Wilberforce had foreseen this, though, and took a pragmatic approach, knowing that the campaign would have to take things one step at a time. Thus, slavery continued throughout much of the British Empire for many years more until August 1833, when a further act was passed which absolutely abolished slavery for good, or as I said earlier, it did so in the eyes of the law. Unfortunately, Wilberforce died in July 1833, just days before this act was passed, although he did live long enough to know that he had finally succeeded in his life's work.

The Wilberforce Way Walk came into being on the 200th anniversary of the 1807 act. The brainchild of a methodist minister called Inderjit Bhogal, who was helped by a man called John Eckersley, the path follows a 60-mile route which can be walked in either direction, although the suggested start is in Hull, probably so you can get the city bit over and done with. The route takes in many places important in the life of Wilberforce, but also some places that are actually very interesting in their own right.

As I've already mentioned, we will walk in the opposite direction, from York to Hull, with *we* being myself and my good friend Rob of course, but there is a good reason for this. We are from Hull, and as you will find out, we're all a bit awkward, and we like to do things differently. And another reason is that we will be walking home, which is always good.

And that home would be Hull, of course. Don't underestimate this fine little Yorkshire city, as it has more history than you could shake a stick at, and there is also lots to learn along the way. For instance, there's a suicidal batman, secret agents, Vikings, battlegrounds, giants and much more besides, so if you're ready, then it is time to begin.

Never Eat a Mole

York to Sutton-upon-Derwent

Today, my son came to me and gave me a hug, totally out of the blue. I was very pleasantly surprised until I heard him tell his mum, '*You're right. He has put weight on.*' This was all I had to hear to know that I had made the right decision to go for a walk today.

As usual, we had somehow picked one of the nicest days imaginable to start the Wilberforce Way. We are lucky like that, and I often wondered if either Rob or myself are, in fact, a weather god, as we always seemed to find ourselves walking on rather nice days.

We'd had a good chat on the way here, discussing the day ahead of us and also sharing our life advice with each other. We had not seen each other for a while, and we had a bit of catching up to do.

For instance, as is usual when we meet up, we tend to discuss our better halves and share hints and tips for maintaining a happy, healthy marriage. Today, Rob told me one of the little secrets he had recently shared with his two young sons. When a woman says something like *'Do what you want,'* seriously, don't do what you want. Stand as still as a statue. Play dead. No blinking. Nothing.

In return, I shared one of my little bits of wisdom. Sick of your other half complaining about your messy house? Just tell him or her that you maintain an alternative lifestyle.

Rob had another corker. Do you find yourself really needing those extra few hours in bed on a Saturday morning? But do the kids keep waking you up? The solution is simple. Just tell them, *'OK kiddos, wake me up in half an hour so we can finally get cracking on cleaning the house from top to bottom.'* Works every time, apparently.

I listened in awe and told Rob he should become a guru, and I knew then that I was really going to enjoy this walk.

The sun shone all around us as we stood at one end of the Wilberforce Way. Depending on which way you choose to travel, it either starts or finishes directly in front of York Minster, the ridiculously impressive cathedral that sits right in the middle of one of the most beautiful cities in England. We were choosing to start our walk here, though there is nothing to stop you from walking in the opposite direction and having this impressive gothic style monster greet you at the end of your walk instead. For us, though, this was to be a walk home, and it is the first time we have ever done a walk which would actually take us home, so it should be interesting.

Our route, then, would take us through the city centre and south along the River Ouse for a while before turning east and wandering through Heslington and the university, where we would then say goodbye to York completely. A hop, a skip and a jump would then lead us past one or two golf courses and towards Wheldrake before a quick diversion through some muddy farmer's fields would land us in Sutton-upon-Derwent. After this, a rather lengthy canal walk would guide us into Pocklington, a somewhat nice but slightly unassuming little gem, after which we would have our first encounter with the rolling hills of the Yorkshire Wolds, so loved by famous artist David Hockney.

Quaint and quiet little villages with names such as Nunburnholme and Londesborough would take us on to Market Weighton, which is yet another incredibly pleasant little town. After this, more hills would beckon as we headed up to Goodmanham, where we would join a disused railway line that would lead us quickly and efficiently towards Beverley, though with brief diversions into the tiny villages of Etton and Cherry Burton.

Beverley itself is an interesting place, and this walk would have us slice straight through the town, which cannot be a bad thing at all, I imagine. More field-hopping would follow, after which the River Hull would snake us into the city of the same name and, of course, bring us home. Finally, we would arrive on the banks of the mighty Humber, which would mark the end of this most interesting walk, and hopefully, by then, we would have learned all sorts of interesting stuff along the way and met some rather interesting people.

I suggested to Rob that we grab a quick photo to mark the start of our walk, so we wandered over to an old column just because it seemed like a good spot to stand. The impressive minster would be behind us, which would obviously make for a nice backdrop. As we stared into my camera, grinning and shouting cheese, commuters and passers-by smiled at us, though this was probably more out of pity than anything else. Perhaps they wondered if we had recently escaped from somewhere official, or were maybe homeless, or even just a couple of simpletons. Perhaps we were.

It is with some amazement, then, that by the time we had taken our first little photograph, we had already encountered enough history to fill an entire chapter, but then we must remember that this is York, and people have been living here for a very long time and have left all sorts of beautiful buildings behind for us to stand in front of nowadays saying things like cheese or boobies.

The first thing was, of course, the column. On it was a plaque informing the humble reader that it had once stood in the headquarters of the Sixth Legion of the Roman army and that it was found here by a bunch of hippy-clad archaeologists in 1969. Okay, it didn't say that, but it was definitely 1969, so they were probably hippies nonetheless. It also told us that York was founded in AD 71, making it very old indeed, even older than my good friend Rob.

Just a few yards from the column was another plaque. This one told us that none other than Constantine the Great was proclaimed Roman Emperor nearby in the year 306, and there was a rather nice statue of him next to it. It must be great, if you pardon the pun, to have such a suffix after your name. I'm not sure what made Constantine so great, but anyway, I was reminded of something that a friend had told me some months back. The conversation had turned to politics, in particular, the recent politics of the Anglo-Saxon nations and the somewhat controversial nature of our current and recent prime ministers and presidents. Anyway, my friend had reminded me that empires were ruled by emperors, kingdoms were ruled by kings, and countries were ruled by, well, I'm sure you can guess the rest.

Anyway, York seems a strange place for anyone to be proclaimed emperor of the Roman Empire, I am sure you will agree. It certainly is a long way from Rome, which begs the question, why here? Well, Constantine had, in fact, accompanied his dad Constantius Chlorus to Britain purely and simply to kill a few Picts up in the frozen north that was Scotland. They had been causing a certain amount of trouble for the Romans, so Constantius decided that if you wanted a job done properly, you had to do it yourself.

Retiring to York for the winter after their northern rampage, which at the time was called Eboracum, Constantius said he didn't feel very well, which was perhaps something of an understatement because he promptly dropped dead, a very long way from home indeed. Just before he popped his clogs, and while on his deathbed, he recommended to his generals that once he had shuffled off this mortal coil, his own son should take over, which is exactly how Constantine the Great found himself becoming emperor here, about as far from Rome as you could get at the time, it has to be said.

Incidentally, Constantine's mum, Helena, was quite famous in her own right, and it is supposedly her who found something called the true cross, which is allegedly the cross that Jesus was crucified on. Legend has it that she also found the nails of the crucifixion, which, you would think, were presumably still nailed into the cross, but anyway, they were said to have miraculous powers, so she had one of them placed in Constantine's helmet as protection, with another in the bridle of his horse. With an advantage like that, then, it is perhaps little wonder that he became so great.

But why is he considered great? Well, until he came along, the Roman empire had been gradually becoming more and more fractured. It was Constantine, then, who managed to unite the whole of the empire under one ruler. He slowly consolidated and extended his power, and within twenty years, he was the sole authority. He became so powerful that he even abandoned Rome, setting up his new capital in what is now modern-day Turkey and naming it after himself. Well, why not? Anyway, Constantinople became the new seat of power, and although it is now known as Istanbul, it is still a very important city to this day, literally bridging two continents, Europe and Asia.

As for the statue, it has been here since the late 1990s, but a few years ago, some cheeky scoundrel stole his sword and chucked it into a drain, and a new one had to be fitted. I hope they've welded this one on a bit better than the last.

As I said, this is a heck of a lot of history, especially when considering we had only taken a couple of dozen steps, but we were not done yet. Just a few steps more took us onto a street called High Petergate, which was on the other side of the smaller church of St Michael, which was itself next to the Minster. On High Petergate, you see, a small pub called, perhaps not surprisingly, The Guy Fawkes Inn, is allegedly the birthplace of none other than Guy Fawkes himself.

Famous, of course, for the Gunpowder Plot, which was the ultimately doomed plan to blow up the Houses of Parliament, Fawkes was said to have been born here way back in 1570. Others, however, say he was born just around the corner, on nearby Stonegate, where there is indeed another plaque, but not a blue one. The truth is that all of the buildings from that era have gone anyway, so we shall probably never know for sure, but he was certainly born around here somewhere, though what we do know for sure is that he was baptised in St Michael's Church, next to the minster. And while his proper name was Guy, he much preferred to be called Guido. It is this name he used to sign his confession when he was ultimately caught trying to do some very naughty things.

Why Fawkes became so well-linked to the plot is perhaps odd, as he was certainly not the ringleader. That would be Robert Catesby, although it was Fawkes who was caught red-handed underneath the House of Lords, with a lantern in one hand and an unlit fuse in the other, which perhaps helps explain why he was the one that became so famous. You can still see the lantern, by the way, as it is on display at a museum in Oxford. Incidentally, the king at the time, King James, described Fawkes as having a 'Roman resolution', which is curious when you think of the Roman links to his birthplace.

Quickly sentenced to death, Fawkes knew his fate would not be good. On the day of his intended execution, he was forced to watch some of his co-conspirators as they were hanged, drawn and quartered. But what did it mean to be hanged, drawn and quartered? Well, it wasn't good, put it that way. First of all, you would be hanged almost to the point of death. Notice the *almost* there, which is crucially important, and which, of course, means you would technically still be alive and therefore very much able to feel pain.

You would then have your penis and testicles removed, at which point you would probably start to question your life choices. Anyway, that would certainly wake you up, which would be useful in making you feel the pain from the next stage, where you would be disembowelled. Not quite key-hole surgery, disembowelling nonetheless means the removal of your intestinal tract through a horizontal slit in your abdomen. If that doesn't kill you, then the next bit will, because this is the bit when they remove your head. After that, your limbs are next, which means that the powers that be now have several bits of you to stick on bridges, gates and spikes, just in case anyone else should get any funny ideas about not paying their taxes or sticking two fingers up at the king.

Anyway, Fawkes managed to avoid all of this, as, on the day of his intended execution, he either fell or deliberately jumped from the gallows ladder and died instantly when he broke his neck. They still chopped him up, though, which kind of defeats the object considering he was already dead, but never mind.

As for the failed plot itself, this has at least given us Brits the opportunity to do stupid things with fireworks every November, and to this very day, the Houses of Parliament are still searched by the Yeomen of the Guard, just in case any nutters with explosives are hiding in the cellars. The actual cellar where Fawkes was caught, however, no longer exists. It was destroyed in the massive fire of 1834 that destroyed the medieval Houses of Parliament, which I think is a bit of a shame.

And finally, it is with quite some irony that every year, thousands more people are injured every bonfire night than on the actual original bonfire night itself, way back in 1605. Burns and scalds are the most common injuries, though there are some truly serious contenders for the Darwin Awards for Stupidity, which apparently occurs every year at exactly the same time as Bonfire night. For instance, a teenager recently had his fingers amputated when a rocket he was holding and which he had just ignited, exploded after just a few seconds. Well, surprise, surprise.

In another *unexpected* incident, a young mum caught fire after pouring petrol on a fire. Who would have thought? But perhaps the best example, and I use the word best in a very particular context here, is that of a young Scot who thought it might be good to launch a firework from between his bare buttocks. Once lit, the firework refused to launch and instead burned fiercely across both of his cheeks. When he attempted to run away, the firework still refused to budge, and in the video clip that I watched, which had racked up around ten thousand views, the hapless victim can be heard begging for a cold shower. By the way, around a thousand of those views were down to me because I just couldn't help myself and had to watch it repeatedly, with the laughter only getting worse with every viewing.

Before we left the square, there was something that we had not really talked about, which could perhaps be described as the elephant in the room, and that elephant was York Minster. There are many things that could be said about it, such as the world-famous 500-year-old rose window, which alludes to the union of the houses of Lancaster and York, and lots of other interesting but boring facts. Instead, I will tell you that somewhere within this giant church, if you look hard enough, you will find carvings of a couple of Star Trek characters, namely a Ferengi and a Klingon, if you know what they are. Surely that's more interesting than what proper guidebooks tell you? If you want to go and search for them, head for the great west doorway, but good luck, because they're tiny.

And after the Minster was struck by lightning in 1984 and subsequently caught fire, Blue Peter, a well-known children's television program at the time, held a competition for design ideas for a rebuild. As a result of this, if you head for the south transept and look up, you will see, among other things, a depiction of Neil Armstrong's first steps on the moon. Take your binoculars, though, as you will need them.

And lastly, on this at least, York Minster is unusual in one other way. There are only two churches in the world with their own police force. One, as you may already know, is St Peter's Basilica in Rome, where the Swiss Guard will promptly sort out any unruly scallywags should they need to. But I bet you didn't know that York Minster also has its own police force, which came about after a man called Jonathan Martin set fire to the building in 1829. This act of arson was probably avoidable, in retrospect anyway, as Martin had already threatened to shoot the Bishop of Oxford a few years before and had spent time in a lunatic asylum as a result.

After serving his time and after the death of his wife, he remarried and moved to York, where at some point, he became annoyed about a buzzing sound he heard coming from the organ inside the Minster. Hiding inside the building on the evening of the 1st of February 1829, he lit his fire later that night, which was not noticed until the next morning, by which time it had become a raging inferno. It took more than twenty-four hours to extinguish the flames, but by then, a huge part of the building was a smouldering ruin, including the organ, the medieval choir stalls, the bishop's throne, and the pulpit. Martin probably would have gotten away with it apart from one teeny, tiny detail. A few days before his heinous act, he had left several threatening placards tied to the railing outside, and on these placards, the moron had written his name and address and had also said he was going to burn the place down.

To stop any further acts of this type and to protect the minster in general, the Minster Police was formed. It is perhaps interesting to note that the Dean of York Minster at the time, a man called William Cockburn, was married to the sister of Sir Robert Peel, who later went on to found the Metropolitan Police. It's a small world, isn't it?

It was time to go, and we left St Michael's and the minster behind, making our way through the throng of tourists that was beginning to gather around us. As I said, York is a very historic city, and we could literally spend all day here, and more besides. But alas, if we wished to make progress on our little walk, that was simply impossible, but there were just a couple of things I wanted to mention before we left. The first is that York is also the final resting place of a famous outlaw, Dick Turpin, and the second is the Lloyds Bank Coprolite. While I am fairly certain that the first of those is self-explanatory, I feel I may need to mention that the second, in case you didn't know, is a rather famous though a rather unlikely piece of fossilised human poo, which is, at the time of writing, on display at the Jorvik Viking Centre. You are welcome.

The term coprolite, by the way, was coined by a man called William Buckland, who devoted much of his life to the study of poo, and he went so far as to have the top of his dining table inlaid with the stuff. That table still exists and is on display at a museum in Lyme Regis, and it is colloquially known as the *poo table* and is quite popular with children. I took my kids, but I have to say that they thought it was a bit shit.

We moved north on High Petergate, passing an array of tourist shops selling all sorts of useless tat that always seems to look better in the store than at home, and escaped the city centre as we passed beneath Bootham Bar. This was the site of one of the four main entrances to the old Roman settlement of Eboracum, although the bar itself is not of Roman construction and was probably built around the 14th century, with the archway itself built slightly earlier. In 1501, a door knocker was installed on the gate, as there was a law at the time that compelled Scottish people to knock and ask the mayor if it was okay to come into the city, I kid you not. In fact, up until recently, it was said that it was still legal to kill a Scotsman in York with a bow and arrow, so long as it wasn't a Sunday. However, if said Scotsman was drunk, then you could kill him anytime, even if it was a Sunday, although in that case, you absolutely and positively could not use a bow and arrow. Anyway, I shouldn't have to say this, but this is all tosh. According to The Law Commission, murder is murder, so don't get any funny ideas if you hear a funny accent while wandering through York.

And before you have a go at us Brits, there are some equally crazy laws from all around the world. For instance, in Indonesia, the penalty for masturbation is decapitation, which begs the question, *how would they know*? In Switzerland, it is illegal for a man to urinate standing up once it is past 10pm, but again, how would they know? And perhaps my favourite is the fact that in France, it is illegal to name a pig Napoleon. Priceless.

We passed beneath the bar and risked life and limb crossing a busy intersection. I probably should have waited for the traffic lights to stop the rather large tourist bus that nearly turned me into a pancake, but I was feeling footloose and fancy-free, and anyway, I made it, just. Those buses have very loud horns, though.

This was Exhibition Square, home to the art gallery as well as a very nice statue of someone who looked rather dapper, and it was all a hive of activity today. Buses were coming and going every few minutes, and small crowds gathered, waiting to go on one walking tour or another around this fine city. I had done one of these myself, many years before, though that one had been a ghost walk. It had ended very badly indeed when me and my friends got simultaneously bored and drunk, having gone to the pub on an empty stomach, a mistake

I shall try not to make again. However, I am certainly not making any promises. The perhaps inevitable conclusion that night had involved traffic cones and policemen, and I have rarely visited this place since then, I should point out.

Anyway, the square was created in the late 1800s, which is when the art gallery was built. We're not going in there today, though. However, it might be worth it just to see the paintings of William Etty. He is, in fact, the person depicted by the statue that stands proudly in front of the gallery and in the centre of the square.

William Etty, you see, is perhaps one of York's most famous sons, and he has a rather strong link to my home city of Hull. Born in York, he moved to my neck of the woods when he was still just a young lad. I am not saying my city corrupted him or anything, but shortly after this, he became rather obsessed with painting pictures of naked ladies. Maybe there was something in the water? He spent seven long years in Hull, and it is fair to say that he considered every last second of his life there as not very nice, to put it mildly. He recalls watching the clock slowly tick by for years on end until midday on the 23rd of October 1805, when he was finally emancipated from his life of *servitude and slavery*, which brings to mind William Wilberforce and his struggle against actual slavery.

Almost every picture that Etty painted contained at least one nude, which caused much controversy at the time and led to him acquiring a reputation for indecency, although we should put this into context and remember that there were rather a lot of old fuddy-duddies around at the time, with a fuddy-duddy being someone who is old fashioned and fussy, just in case you are not from around these parts.

The fact that Etty enjoyed painting the beauty of the human body was perhaps odd, as, and I am afraid there is no easy way to say this, he was rather ugly, and this is not just my opinion. His biographer was a man called Alexander Gilchrist, who was also the biographer of famous poet and painter William Blake. Gilchrist was, in fact, the person who wrote what is considered to be *the* standard reference work about one of England's greatest ever poets, so based on this, we can probably trust what he said about Etty being as ugly as a toad.

Of Etty, then, Gilchrist described him as slovenly in attire with a big fat head and an ugly face. I'm paraphrasing, of course, but he really did paint a rather negative picture of him, saying he was, and I'm actually quoting now, *one of the oddest-looking creatures in a young lady's eyes.* However, in a self-portrait from 1823, Etty cuts a dashing and handsome figure indeed and looks almost Shakespearian, but then you wouldn't actually paint yourself as an ugly freak of nature, would you?

He never married but lived much of his life with his niece Betsy. Don't read anything into that, as although he was incredibly attached to her, there is nothing to suggest that anything was going on. Indeed, after living with him for several years, there are indications that Betsy did have one or two relations with men her own age, although she always retained a soft spot for her uncle, and she stayed with him until his death.

Although Etty left York when he was very young, he maintained strong and close links with the city of his birth and was one of the most vocal campaigners to resist plans to modernise York Minster following the arson attack of 1829. Etty campaigned successfully for the building to be restored to its original state, while others suggested a more modernist approach, but thankfully Etty stood his ground, and thank goodness he did, as it's beautiful inside and out.

Quite bizarrely, the Corporation of York, which was basically the city council of the time, also made a proposal to demolish the city walls and modernise the whole town. Etty was once again on the case, and despite painting pictures and giving lectures about the importance of retaining the historic walls, which had already begun attracting tourists even back then, the York and North Midland Railway nonetheless smashed a great big hole through the medieval walls and brought the railway lines right into the heart of the city. Not only was this a sad loss for the place, but it became a pointless one when, just a few years later, a new train station was built just outside of the city walls, where it has remained ever since.

Etty returned to York in later life, and it is where he eventually died, in the city that he loved so much. As part of his legacy, he lobbied for the founding of an art school there, something that eventually came to fruition when the York School of Design opened in 1842. Ironically, with the funds for the school largely coming from Etty and his nude portraits, a complaint from a female art student in 1847 concerning the penises of several replicas of Ancient Greek sculptures saw each and every one of them promptly chopped off, which is, of course, a fate that even Guy Fawkes had managed to avoid. This still caused considerable controversy at the time, and male and female students alike remonstrated against this wanton act of destruction. However, it was already too late, as the choppers had already been chopped.

I'm not sure what Etty thought of this, but I doubt he would have been impressed. He continued painting right up until his death, including a rather impressive set of panels depicting Joan of Arc, although in this case, he painted her with her clothes on. He actually settled permanently back in York just a year or so before his death and had his house remodelled so that he had a commanding view of the River Ouse. It was here that he croaked, with his last words reportedly being *'Wonderful! Wonderful! This death!'*

Etty had planned to be buried in York Minster and could certainly have afforded it, but unfortunately, he forgot to make provision for this in his will. Also unfortunately, the city, and perhaps most of the country, was busy going bankrupt thanks to the nefarious schemings of George Hudson, the Railway King. Etty was therefore buried in the small parish churchyard near where he lived, St Olave's, and perhaps somewhat ironically, he is buried uncomfortably close to a man called Richard Nicholson, who was none other than the brother-in-law of George Hudson himself. Nicholson had died of natural causes, assuming you consider suicide by drowning to be natural causes, that is, as he too had gone bankrupt and was buried within months of Etty.

Etty, despite neglecting his own burial costs in his will, did actually leave rather a lot of money behind, and it is rather telling and somewhat sad that no one chose to pick up the tab for a decent burial within the minster, but such is life I guess, or in this case, such is death.

We left the now bustling square and cut through a narrow path sandwiched in between the old city walls and the Yorkshire Museum. The contrast was extraordinary, and we immediately found ourselves in a secluded and beautiful garden with hardly a soul about.

We ventured over to investigate an old but interesting looking building which seemed to be wearing a pointy hat. It wasn't, of course, it was just the roof, and the building turned out to be the old observatory. A small blue plaque told us that a man called Thomas Cook designed his refracting telescope within this building, and I mentioned to Rob that we had come across this guy before. Cook had been born at Allerthorpe but had worked as the headmaster at Skirpenbeck school, which is where we had first come across him a few years back on one of our many walks.

We had been attempting to walk across England in a dead straight line at a latitude of 54 degrees north, just to see if we could really, and Skirpenbeck is one of the towns and villages that lie exactly at that latitude. I remembered that Cook had originally ground down old whisky tumblers in order to make lenses for his first telescopes, but I had not realised he had done it here, at the York Observatory, though in retrospect, this makes perfect sense. Anyway, he was somewhat successful, and his telescopes were eventually exported all around the world. Amazingly, most of them are still in use today, which is bewildering when you consider they are over 150 years old.

As I moved around the observatory, there was a poster featuring a photograph of John Herschel, which was a surprise as he certainly wasn't local to York.

It turned out, however, that this picture of Herschel was one of a dozen placed around the gardens and the museum that depicted the first known photographs taken in York. This had happened when a couple of pioneers in the world of photography attended a meeting of the British Association for the Advancement of Science, which was held here way back in 1844. This was the second time the group had met here, the first time being in 1831, when the association had actually been founded here, which was news to me. The pioneers in photography, then, were two men called David Octavius Hill and Robert Adamson, who had come down from Scotland specifically to photograph the attendees at this conference using an early form of photography known as a calotype, and which thus gives us some incredibly interesting images of lots of dead people. This is actually pretty amazing, I said to Rob, as many of these photographs were of men born way back in the 1700s, and although I had never really thought about it as such, it is pretty cool that we have pictures of people born so long ago.

Luckily for us, not only was Herschel one of those dead people, but guess who else was? If you said William Etty, then have a merit badge because you are right. I have to say that in his photograph, at least, he does not particularly seem to have a fat head or an ugly face, though he certainly fits the bill when it comes to slovenly attire. There is no mention of his love for nudes either, and he is described simply as one of the most famous painters of his day who campaigned for an art school in York and who worked to protect the city walls. The people who wrote his bio failed to mention breaking penises off statues either, the boring old farts. It's a good job you've got me to get to the interesting stuff, isn't it?

What it did tell us, though, is that we could see Etty's grave nearby, through the railings in the abbey ruins, which were literally just a few yards away.

On the other posters, there were several pictures of other boring looking Victorians, but at least one more caught my eye. This was another William, which was presumably a very common name back then, though this was William Scoresby. It was Robin who was now reminding me that we had come across this guy too, though this had been on the Cleveland

Way when we had been passing through Whitby. Scoresby wouldn't do well nowadays, as he spent most of his time harpooning whales and clubbing baby seals to death, so the animal rights lobby would probably be chopping something of his off, but back in the day, these products were essential.

For instance, it was whale oil that lubricated much of the machinery of the industrial revolution, and without it, we would still be living in shacks and having cabbage soup for dinner. And lunch. And probably breakfast. Scoresby was much more than a whaler, however, as he was also a great explorer as well as a scientist. He followed in the rather big footsteps of his father, also William, who was yet another whaler but who also, according to some accounts, invented the crow's nest, which later became very common on ships.

The photos, by the way, were all taken in an open-air studio just a few yards away in the ruins of St Mary's Abbey, which is exactly where we went next. We soon found the metal gate, behind which was the final resting place of William Etty, and although his grave wasn't in the Minster, obviously, it was still pretty impressive. A rather big sarcophagus was perfectly framed by the ruined walls of the abbey, and upon reflection, this is probably a much more dramatic place to spend eternity than the minster, plus it is in a nice garden with lots of pretty flowers. I know where I'd rather be.

We moved on, leaving the garden under an arched gateway, and turned left towards the river. More city walls adorned our left, or at least I thought they were city walls, though they were rather small and may have just been the garden walls for the abbey.

We were soon at the River Ouse and began to follow it downstream, which was easy, as a wide, tree-lined path made our going as nice as any walk I could imagine taking. Students pedalled briskly past us in both directions, swerving this way and that so as to avoid hitting slower and ploddering walkers such as ourselves, and one swerved so violently towards the water that I almost expected to hear a loud scream followed by an impressive splash a few seconds later. Sadly, he regained his balance, and pedalled on.

I did not know it at the time, but this path was called Dame Judi Dench Walk and was so-named in tribute to one of York's most famous daughters, who was born here in 1934 and which therefore made her much older than I had thought she was. She is perhaps most famous for her role as 'M' in the various James Bond movies, but there are a couple of interesting things about her that are not so well known. Firstly, she was brought up as a quaker, and secondly, and perhaps more interestingly, she once had a Harvey Weinstein tattoo drawn on her backside as a tribute to the help he gave her to launch her career. This was a while back, though, and was certainly well before Weinstein became associated with the many counts of rape and sexual assault that were levelled against him. Luckily for Dench, her tattoo was only a temporary one, which was a pretty close call when you think about it.

A bridge was ahead of us, which we would have to cross, as the path would now take us over to the western side of York for a mile or so. This was Lendal Bridge, and it is rather old, having been built in 1861 when it replaced a ferry service that ran between Lendal Tower and Barker Tower, the two medieval towers that still exist today and which sit right next to the bridge. These towers were not just for defensive purposes, but they were also used to control river traffic entering the city. A huge iron chain would be stretched across the river, and boatmen were forced to pay a toll to cross it. Unfortunately for these boatmen, there was another chain just a few yards up the river at St Mary's Abbey, where they would have to pay yet again, which seems a bit rich when you think about it.

A ferry service also ran between the two towers, which was obviously and immediately put out of business as soon as the bridge opened, but anyone wanting to cross the river would still have to pay to use the bridge, at least when it first opened. The toll booths still sit at each end of the bridge, and we went in the one on the western side, which was now a small cafe, as Rob had foolishly forgotten to bring any lunch, and he certainly wasn't having any of mine.

The greedy little devil actually bought himself two packs of sandwiches, which I just thought was him being a pig, though perhaps he was going to share them with me? While we were there, we had a good chat with the proprietor, who certainly seemed to know the area well, and who told us a bit about the museum gardens we had just come from.

He also told us that Barker Tower, which was the round one on the same side of the river that we were on, was used as the city mortuary when it became obsolete due to the bridge. Lendal Tower, the square one on the other side of the river, became the waterworks for quite some time, but you can now rent it out as a holiday apartment, he informed us. Lastly, he told us that whoever built Lendal Tower stole most of the bricks from St Mary's Abbey, which partly explains why it stands as a ruin today, I guess.

Lendal Bridge itself was built by a man called Thomas Page, who is perhaps more famous for Westminster Bridge, which is the big one that stands right next to the Houses of Parliament in London, and he also came up with one of the first serious ideas for a channel tunnel, proposing a submerged tube, though ultimately this plan came to nothing.

After our little chat, and with Rob's backpack now stuffed with food, we moved on, following nondescript little streets through the centre of York, though I couldn't help but think that we were on the wrong side of the river and that most of the interesting stuff was on the other side. We passed bus stops and shops and cafes, but nothing of any real interest, so we headed for Skeldergate Bridge, where we would cross back over to the right side, although I did get side-tracked at the next bridge, which was the Ouse Bridge.

I popped to the centre of this one to take a photo, and on the way back, I noticed a metal plaque. It was at a very low height, but then it had to be really as the walls of the bridge were not very tall, but anyway, it told any passing four-year-olds, and possibly Rob's wife, who is also vertically challenged, that Margaret Clitheroe was executed not far from this spot. To be honest, I had actually heard of this story before, and the plaque could have been a bit more imaginative, it has to be said, such is the richness of the story that surrounds her.

What actually happened to her, you see, was as follows, but first, a bit of background. Margaret was a Catholic who lived in a time when being a Catholic was not really the best thing that you could possibly be. Anyway, she refused to hide her faith, and despite being married to a protestant herself, she still used a secret room in her house for private meetings of all things Catholic, as well as for hiding the odd priest. I don't mean that she hid priests that were odd, of course, though I'm sure some of them probably were. I mean, you do tend to get a bit paranoid when all of society wants to either hang you by the gizzard or put you on the top of a nice, warm fire.

Anyway, Margaret was charged with hiding a priest but refused to plea. As a result, she was swiftly sentenced to death, something that was carried out on this very bridge, just next to the toll booth. Her method of execution was an odd one, though, to us modern humans at least, although it was perfectly normal at the time. Margaret, you see, was crushed beneath her own front door, taken from her house on the Shambles, one of the prettiest streets in York. The door was brought here and placed on top of her, after which rocks were placed on top of it until she was well and truly dead. Quite sadly, she had been pregnant with her fourth child at the time. Her death became the most infamous example of this most barbaric practice, which was finally abandoned in 1772, though this was much too late for poor Margaret Clitheroe, of course.

And don't go thinking that this type of death was necessarily a quick one. Pressing to death often took several days and was not always done with an increasing load, as not adding extra weight would actually prolong the agony for the person in question. To illustrate this, John Weekes, who was killed by this method in 1731, refused to plead and endured a slow and agonising torture and was only killed when bystanders sat on him as an act of mercy. In another example, Giles Corey, who was pressed to death between the 17th and the 19th of September 1692, enduring around 48 hours of unimaginable agony in the process, perhaps surprised all present when they heard his last words, which were said to be '*more weight*'.

Margaret went on to become one of the *Forty Martyrs of England and Wales*, a rather select club if ever there was one. This group was made up of Catholics of all backgrounds executed between 1535 and 1679, a particularly bad time to be a Catholic clearly, and many were killed with only a show trial, hence the regular reluctance to make a plea, and in some extreme cases, no trial at all.

The best bit of this story is coming up, though, and it is even crazier than what we have just heard. You see, many years before, on a ghost tour of The Shamble, where Margaret Clitheroe had lived, a tour guide related the story of her life and the rather gory details of her death, and then she told me that, if I wanted, I could go and see Margaret's hand, which was sort of mummified and on display in a convent in the city. Did I go and see it? Hell, yeah, of course I bloody did.

I practically ran through York city centre, all the way to the Bar Convent, where some rather scary nuns greeted a rather sweaty tourist with beads of perspiration dripping down his neck and who appeared to be having a heart attack, having run across the city at some speed and with some peril, having had several near misses with open-topped tour buses and at least one rather speedy tuk-tuk.

Anyway, I don't think they had a lot of visitors in those days, and while their customer service skills were not what you would call great, they did show us in and sat us down in front of a fancy velvet curtain. In a complete and spooky silence, one of the nuns slowly pulled a rope, which opened the curtain and revealed the mummified hand of Margaret Clitheroe. It was contained within a glass dome surrounded by fancy metalwork, and her hand seemed to have been chopped off just as she was waving goodbye, such was the pose it was in. It was all a bit weird and surreal and is yet another one of those tourist attractions that the powers that be don't tell you about but which they really should.

Perhaps luckily for Margaret, she died within fifteen minutes, but they left the rocks on top of her for a good few hours, just to make sure. Ironically, perhaps, she was executed on Lady Day in 1586, which also happened to be Good Friday. Lastly, and perhaps not surprisingly, St Margaret is the patron saint of expectant mothers.

Moving on, and only a few yards from the Ouse Bridge, we stopped for another minute to look at the incredibly pretty scene on the other side of the river. Cobbled streets and a mix of colourful buildings, including the King's Arms pub, formed a very nice picture indeed, and it is perhaps not difficult to believe that this is one of the most flooded places in Britain when you see its incredibly low level in comparison to the river. Indeed, within the pub, there are marks on the wall showing the height that the floodwaters have reached over the years, with the floods appearing to happen on an uncomfortably regular basis.

Although we weren't going in today, Rob and I had been in there a while back and had enjoyed a couple of pints. It had been very busy, but we managed to find a couple of seats right at the end of the bar. I must admit that this had not been the first pub we had visited that day, and it certainly wasn't the last either. As we were leaving, I noticed two drunks across from us, pointed them out, and said to Rob, *'That's us in ten years,'* to which he replied, *'That's a mirror.'*

If this bit of York looks familiar to you, too, then it might be because you are a fan of Garfield. In his 2006 movie *A Tale of Two Kitties*, it is over there on those cobbles where the precocious moggy almost manages to get himself squashed by a car. However, in the scene, York is imitating London, and it does a very good job, even if I do say so myself. For some reason, though, the producers of the film tried to make the whole scene look a bit more British with the addition of a letterbox and a phone box, though I'm not sure why, as looking across there now, the scene is about as quintessentially English as you could possibly get.

We arrived at Skeldergate Bridge, which was another one of Thomas Page's designs, but unfortunately, Page died early on in the construction, so his son George took over. This was another toll bridge, and once again, the toll booth seems to have been turned into a coffee shop or café, but this bridge had another trick up its sleeve. The north-eastern part was designed to open to allow tall ships to pass, which it did for many years, although it has not opened since 1975, and the winding mechanism has now been removed. Still, it is a very nice bridge.

This reminds me of another bridge, which, while not related to this one, is quite a funny story. It concerns the Sean O'Casey Bridge, which is a pedestrian swing bridge spanning the River Liffey in Dublin. This was a state-of-the-art bridge when it was completed in 2005, and it had a fantastic feature that meant you didn't even have to be on the bridge to operate the opening mechanism when a ship or boat came along, as there was a remote control.

All was great until sometime in 2010 when someone lost the remote. You would have thought they might have had a spare, but they had instead decided to save a bit of money and only had the one. They looked down the back of the settee, they looked in the bin, and they even looked in the fridge, but the remote control was nowhere to be seen. Unfortunately, because of the type of remote control, which was simply described as bespoke, you couldn't just go online and order a replacement. As a consequence, the bridge couldn't be opened for the next four years, which was when they finally managed to get another remote, and at which point I expect they found the original remote, probably at the back of the cupboard where it had been all along and where they had already looked twice.

Back to Thomas Page, though, and although I never managed to find out what he died of, I did learn that he snuffed it suddenly while in Paris, so I do hope he was having a good time partying and whatnot and not doodling out yet another boring design for a triple-arched bridge or whatever, but obviously, we will never know.

As well as his many bridges, Page should also be remembered for something else, but alas, it is something that is almost forgotten. During the early part of his career, he worked for Edward Blore, a gothic architect who clearly influenced much of Page's later work, including these bridges in York, of course. Blore tasked Page with the job of conducting a thorough survey of Westminster Abbey, and during the process of this, he accidentally rediscovered a previously forgotten passage that ran from the transept to the crypt of the Chapter House.

In doing so, Page also inadvertently discovered Britain's oldest door, which has recently been dated using the process of dendrochronology, where wood can be dated using the characteristic patterns of annual growth rings in timber or tree trunks. Analysis showed that the timber used for this door was from an oak tree cut down sometime after 1032 AD, and the door itself was constructed sometime in the 1050s. Fast forward to the 19th century, fragments of cowhide were also noted on the door, but a legend grew that it was actually human skin taken from someone who had been caught committing sacrilege or robbery and whose skin had been flayed and nailed to the door as a deterrent to others. Nice.

Rob decided that he had to go and find a toilet, despite me telling him that he should have gone before we set off, and sometimes I think it is like trying to deal with a child who just will not listen. While he did so, I sat on a bench and watched joggers and cyclists flying by. I noticed that almost every one of them was rather portly, which perhaps explained why they were currently engaged in such strenuous activities.

Before you have a go at me and start going on about body shaming and all that, allow me to mention that I am also becoming rather portly. In fact, I am becoming increasingly so almost every day. I seem to have reached that age where it is incredibly easy to pile the pounds on, which seems to happen simply by looking at things such as cakes and ice creams, while it is far harder to then get rid of those exact same pounds. In fact, the latter never happens, and I simply seem to be slowly but surely ballooning into something that is one day going to explode.

Talking of explosions, Rob eventually returned from his expedition, and it had taken that long that I suspected he had created yet another coprolite. Anyway, after putting his rucksack back on, we carried on with our walk. This section of the riverside path was pretty busy, with people whizzing about on scooters and bicycles, but unfortunately, not a single one of them fell off, crashed, or did anything at all remotely interesting or entertaining, which was a real shame. There is nothing like someone else's disaster to put a smile on your face, but maybe I just haven't properly grown up.

The path was straight and long, or at least it seemed to be long, but Rob said that maybe it was just the company that made it seem like that, which was a bit of a cheek.

We did stop for a moment and gaze across the river, and I told him that over there was the site of an old convent, namely St Clementhorpe, that had quite a lot of interesting history. That story would have to wait until we got to Beverley though, as the tale was intricately linked with the place. I tried to get Rob on tenterhooks about this most interesting tale, but he just yawned as he walked off, which was not quite what I had intended.

Presently we came to a small iron bridge, Blue Bridge, which was, as its name suggests, very blue indeed. I guess they just couldn't think of what to call it, and as *Bridge of the Gods* was already taken, Blue Bridge it was. I once remember watching a documentary about how they built this bridge. It was riveting.

This small bridge took us over the River Foss, which ended its journey here, or at least where it blended its journey with that of its larger cousin, the Ouse. A flood barrier was visible just a few yards to our north, which closes whenever river levels in the Ouse get uncomfortably high, which is probably quite often. York has long been a victim of flooding, and I guess it always will be, especially if current trends continue.

We took a quick diversion here, leaving the Wilberforce Way behind for a while, and headed to Dick Turpin's grave at St George's graveyard near Lead Mill Lane. It was only a short walk of a few minutes, and I promised Rob that it would definitely be worth the deviation, and when we got there, we were richly rewarded. A small grass oasis in the heart of the city was the final resting place for this notorious highwayman, although on his gravestone was his other name, which was John Palmer.

Turpin started his career as a butcher but quickly turned to crime when he fell in with the wrong crowd. I asked Rob if that was his excuse, too, but he just laughed. Turpin did some truly terrible things, yet we seem to remember him as this romanticised highwayman of old. What we forget is that he killed his own partner, poured scalding water on someone he disliked, and threw another person onto a fire while they were still alive.

Anyway, he was finally captured after a fight over a chicken, eventually brought here to be put on trial, and when his true identity was revealed, he was executed by hanging right here in York. I told you it would be worth it.

We re-traced our steps and carried on heading south. After a few yards, Rob stopped and went to stare at a wall, which I thought was a bit odd, and for a moment or two, I wondered if he had maybe had a stroke. I was all set to abandon him and move on and figured I would just tell his wife I had lost him when he beckoned me over to look at something.

What he had actually found was a small plaque on the wall, though how he had noticed it was beyond me. The plaque informed us that this spot was the site of a narrow-gauge railway that was previously used to bring bullets and bombs into the barracks that also once stood here. Boats would pull up on the riverbank, and soldiers would load their deadly cargo into small carts that would then be hauled into the ordnance depot, and this all went on up until the 1950s. After I had read this, I turned around and lo and behold, I found a couple of little railway tracks that led straight to the water's edge, although they were now somewhat covered in silt. You learn something every day.

Something else I learned about the River Ouse is that its name is a bit silly and is something called a tautology. Allow me to explain.

Ouse derives from the Celtic languages that were spoken on our little island before the Anglo-

Saxons came along, with the actual Celtic word being Usa, which derived from Udso, which literally meant wet or water, but which was also derived from a generic word used for a river. When you think about it, then, the literal translation of River Ouse is river river, which, as I said, is a bit stupid but is a result of new arrivals adopting foreign words without knowing their actual meaning. Anyway, that is what a tautology is, basically saying the same thing twice but with different words.

Another example of this type of tautology is Pendle Hill, a rather large mountain on the other side of Yorkshire and which is actually an excellent example of a triple tautology. Pen means hill, you see, but this did not stop later arrivals from changing its name to Pendle, which made it hill hill. So calling it Pendle Hill as we do nowadays actually means you are calling it hill hill hill.

But the best example has to be Torpenhow Hill near the tiny village of Torpenhow in Cumbria. Over the years, its name morphed into its current form, with tor, pen and how all meaning hill in different ancient languages, old English, Welsh and Norse, respectively. Our modern addition makes the name of this supposed hill to actually be hill hill hill hill, which is completely crackers.

This is supposed to be an excellent example of a tautology, but I say supposed as it appears that while this is a great story and a good example of a quadruple tautology, there is no hill near the village of Torpenhow, so how this myth came to become the legend that it has is unclear.

Other interesting examples include Lake Tahoe, which is simply *lake lake*, as well as the Sahara Desert, which translates to *deserts desert*. The famous El Camino Way actually means *the way way*, and even our very own Milky Way Galaxy actually translates as *milky way milky*, as galaxy is derived from the Greek word galaxias, which means milky.

My favourite by far, though, and I promise this will be the last one, is the La Brea Tar Pits in Los Angeles. La Brea is Spanish for *the tar,* so La Brea Tar Pits is actually *the tar tar pits*. However, we're not done yet, as it gets even better. On the website of this popular attraction, it is actually referred to as *The La Brea Tar Pits*, which literally means *the the tar tar pits*. You couldn't make it up.

Sadly, it was time to leave the river behind us, and Rob was bored of talking about tautologies. We turned left and followed a track that led through an industrial estate, passing lots of companies that I had never heard of. After crossing a main road, we entered a much more unusual environment, as we appeared to be walking right through the middle of an army base. High barbed wire fences caged us in from either side, and through this fence, we could see an assortment of land rovers and trucks, as well as one rather impressive beast that looked as if it had spent quite a lot of time in the desert doing something rather naughty.

A sign warned of tanks crossing ahead of us, which seemed unlikely in the extreme, bearing in mind we were still firmly in the suburbs of a relatively small English city, but just a few yards further on, a vehicle was waiting at a large metal gate. It wasn't actually a tank, but inside were a couple of soldiers who seemed to be keeping a firm eye on us. The problem was, though, they looked too young. One of them could barely see over the steering wheel, and they looked so fresh-faced it was almost ridiculous. I am used to seeing this at my son's school, as the teachers all look really young nowadays, but I had never encountered this phenomenon when it came to soldiers before. I really must be getting old, I told myself.

Leaving barbed wire fences and things that go bang behind us, we entered a pleasant meadow, where the sound of a diesel engine was replaced with the singing of a bird. Several oldies beavered busily away on allotments to our left, presumably preparing them for the coming spring, as I suggested to Rob that there were not many plants ready to harvest in what was essentially still the middle of winter, even if it was a really nice, sunny day. Walkers and cyclists passed us, including one little old lady who pedalled so slowly that she almost seemed to be defying gravity in not having fallen over. She was barely going any faster than what we were walking, and we actually kept up with her for quite a while after she had passed us.

We had arrived at the university, where she turned right, and we went left, and it seemed strange that a long-distance footpath would take us through such a place.

It was positively buzzing today, and students scurried this way and that, presumably on their way to one pub or another. And please don't try to tell me otherwise. I've been a student myself, so I know how it works.

You would expect an ancient city such as York to have a fine old university, perhaps one that was hundreds of years old. Alas, this is not the case, and to be honest, you can probably tell this by simply poking around the site, which we did now as we passed through. Many buildings seemed thoroughly modern, especially at the western end, and as we walked towards the east, the buildings gradually seemed to get slightly older, but only very slightly. The oldest ones seemed to have a pedigree of the 1960s, as indeed they should, as this was when the university was founded, which seems far too recent if you ask me.

Anyway, the university first flung open its doors in 1963, and a frenzied period of activity saw these older buildings going up remarkably quickly. Heslington Hall, an old manor house, initially formed the university's heart, and another nice feature was a rather large lake. This wasn't for aesthetics, however, but was because the land around here was so boggy and marshy that they had to build somewhere for the water to drain off to, otherwise, all the students would have wet feet.

The 1970s was the period when the place really came to life, hosting bands such as The Who, Hot Chocolate and other top-flight performers of the day such as Acker Bilk and John Williams. Paul McCartney even turned up one day with his wife Linda and performed an impromptu concert in one of the dining rooms, which must have been ace.

The 1980s were not so good. Government funding cuts impacted heavily on the place, to the point where staff were asked to turn the thermostats down, wear woolly hats, and keep their phone calls as short as possible in order to save money. On top of this, the chemistry department burned down, which was probably very dramatic but not good in the scheme of things, though at least the staff would have been warm for a bit, and to top all of this off, Bob Geldof performed a concert here with his Boomtown Rats. Unfortunately, he told the crowd to come to the front of the auditorium so he could see them all, which ultimately caused over a thousand pounds worth of damage to the orchestra pit cover. Ah, the good old days.

We passed a rather large Buddha, which had been a gift from one ex-student or another, presumably when they realised that they maybe didn't have space for it in their living room after all, and we then crossed a pleasant bridge over the lake. After this, we seemed to leave the university behind. In fact, we soon found ourselves in Heslington, a confused little place that is somewhere between a suburb of York and a village in its own right.

We passed Heslington Hall, which was largely hidden behind high brick walls, and which was, of course, the original university. The house is actually hundreds of years old and has seen a lot of history, and during the Second World War, it was home to Number 4 Group of the Royal Air Force, which comprised several squadrons of bombers. This was initially led by none other than Arthur 'Bomber' Harris, who went on to lead the whole of the RAF by the end of the war. The squadrons in this group became involved in operations as diverse as leaflet dropping at the start of the war to the one thousand bomber raids towards the end. They were also responsible for bombing the German battlecruiser Scharnhorst, an act which helped keep it docked in Brest for some months longer than necessary for essential repairs.

Students still wandered this way and that, almost aimlessly it seemed, although one or two of them really were heading for the pub. We found it ourselves soon enough, and it was confusingly called the Charles XII. I knew that there had never been a king bearing that title, at least not in this country anyway, but the picture on the pub sign provided a more than ample clue. The Charles XII in question was, in fact, a horse, and he was owned by Major Nicholas Yarburgh, who it turns out once owned Heslington Hall.

This horse was apparently legendary in the horse-racing world, winning the renowned St Leger in 1839 in the second race, after the first race was declared a dead heat between Charles XII, nicknamed the *Yorkshire Nag*, and Euclid, the *Newmarket Pet*. This marked the first-ever dead-heat recorded at the St Leger, though there was another a few years later in 1850.

The result of the second race looked to be the same as the first, but at the last minute, Charles XII managed to pull ahead and win by a nose.

Major Yarburgh sold Charles XII in 1840, just a year after his amazing win, but the horse continued its stunning career before being put out to stud in 1843. Of the thirty-four races he ran during his career, he won nineteen of them, and interestingly, the next dead-heat recorded at the St Leger in 1850 involved a horse called Voltigeur, who had shared the same father as Charles XII, a horse named Voltaire.

We wandered south through this sleepy village, which ended abruptly at a sharp bend just a few hundred yards later, where we turned off the road and onto a long, straight track. We had this to ourselves, and with not a soul in sight, we talked about this and that and explained to each other how we would solve all of the world's problems if we were in charge, as us blokes tend to do.

Walking directly into the sun, Rob realised he had forgotten his sunglasses, which I added to the list that had started with his sandwiches, and I wondered what he would realise he had forgotten next. I did suggest we played a game, one similar to *one man went to mow, went to mow a meadow*, where you add items on with every round, although in this case, we could use items that Rob had forgotten to bring today. He wasn't very happy about this, and I won't tell you what he said to me, but the second word was *off*.

We must have become quite engrossed in whatever conversation we were having because in what seemed like no time at all, we were at the southern bypass to the city and passed over it via a bridge that seemed to be hosting a tractor rally. I imagine it had been quiet all day, but as we arrived, several chugging and puffing little engines passed over it one by one, shrouding us in a cloud of Yorkshire's finest smoky diesel fumes, for which we were eternally grateful.

On the other side of the road, the landscape changed from the patchwork of fields we had just been walking through to a perfectly manicured and rather large lawn. A small hut beckoned us over, but as we moved towards it, an unseen voice called us in another direction instead.

Apparently, this place was a golf course, and we had veered several inches away from the public footpath that ran across it, a helpful voice informed us. How we would have known this, it is hard to say, as there was no physical sign of a path and certainly no signposts. Apparently, however, we should be following the white sticks, as these marked the route through the place. Obviously, Rob and I are both incredibly stupid, so we apologised profusely for our ignorance and vowed to follow random white sticks at all times in the future.

However, an actual sign would have been useful, but that is all I am going to say about that. Or, if you are doing this walk yourself and you do not want to get told off by an old fart in baggy trousers and a stupid hat, you could come disguised as a golfer yourself by wearing some silly clothes and an even sillier headpiece, and you will blend right in.

We hobbled along the edge of the golf course, which seemed to go on forever, next to a deep and terrifying ditch. I did wonder what I would do if I suddenly heard someone shout fore, which would signal an incoming projectile of circular proportions, apparently, and considered whether it would be better to hit the deck and cover my head with my hands like those kids do in those propaganda films when a nuclear attack is imminent, or whether it would be more sensible to dive into the ditch and take my chances with the leeches.

Ultimately, I reckoned neither would be particularly conducive to my health and decided instead to keep a couple of steps behind my giant of a walking companion, who would hopefully absorb any impact in the same way that Jupiter has been protecting the Earth for the last few billion years. Did I already mention that Rob is rather tall? And that therefore he makes an excellent bodyguard? I knew there was a reason why I had brought him on this walk, I chuckled to myself as I followed him along, also benefitting from the considerable shade he was providing me from the sun that was still very much dead ahead of us.

Unfortunately, this protection from errant golf balls and solar radiation did not last for long, as Rob wanted to talk, so for the next mile we walked side by side, with him grumbling about the molehills and me grumbling about everything else in general, but sunshine and golf balls in particular.

Looking at our map, we were on Fulford golf course, which is confusingly on Heslington Common. The course seems to straddle the main ring road around York, which is certainly interesting in a *I don't give a fuck about health and safety* sort of way, and I did wonder how many golf balls have woken up sleepy drivers as they made their way to work on autopilot.

Anyway, this spot, or at least somewhere near here, was also the site of the Battle of Fulford way back in 1066. Most people know the story of The Battle of Hastings or have at least heard of it, but not many people have heard about the one at Fulford, which is actually where it all started, sort of.

There were lots of people involved, many of whom had a claim to the throne of England, which had been up for grabs since Edward the Confessor had snuffed it in January of that year. We will concentrate on just a few of them, in particular Harold Godwinson and his brother Tostig, King Harald III of Norway, also known as Harald Hardrada, and a couple of Northern Earls called Edwin as well as his brother Morcar, the Earl of Northumberland.

When Edward the Confessor popped his clogs, Harold Godwinson made a dash for London and claimed the throne. Edwin and Morcar were not too happy about this, as they also wanted it, and although they initially challenged Harold Godwinson, they soon fell in line and backed him as the lesser of two evils. In the meantime, the king's own brother, Tostig, disappeared over the horizon and formed an unholy alliance with Harald Hardrada, as he, too, had his eyes on the throne. According to some historians, Tostig also went to see William, Duke of Normandy, to see if he wanted in on the action. However, it is said that William chose to stay out of things at that time.

To cut a long story short, Hardrada and Tostig formed an army and sailed to Britain, and it is here at Fulford that they had a bit of a scrap with brothers Edwin and Morcar, ultimately beating the living daylights out of them.

Egged on by their quick victory at Fulford, Harald and Tostig moved on towards Stamford Bridge, where a much more famous battle took place a few days later. In that battle, they fought against Tostig's brother Harold Godwinson. Unfortunately, both Harald Hardrada and Tostig Godwinson ended up on the wrong end of something rather sharp, and both of them were killed in this battle, and that was the end of them.

A victorious and newly emboldened Harold Godwinson then made a quick dash for the south coast, as he had heard that some pesky foreigners had just invaded, led by none other than William Duke of Normandy. You may already know what happened at that one, and if you don't, here's a clue: William changed his name after this battle and was forever after known as William the Conqueror, and Harold famously took an arrow in the eye and ended up ever so slightly dead.

You could, in retrospect, think that William had played everyone off against each other and had simply stayed out of the fight until the last round just so that all of the others would have the chance to kill one another, and if this was the case, then it was clearly a very smart move and explains why we are now who we are and why we speak the language we do. These events had, more or less simultaneously, ended the long history of Viking occupation on this island and also ushered in the Norman conquest. Anyway, all of that started right here, and it is a lot more interesting than golf.

Incidentally, Rob tried to fob me off with a story about golf, or more accurately, why golf is called, well, golf. He said it stood for *gentlemen only, ladies forbidden*, and as I looked at him doubtfully, he crossed his heart and hoped to die and all that, professing that he was telling the truth. I had severe doubts, let's just put it at that, and when I asked a good friend of mine, it turned out that this story is indeed absolute bunkum.

It was at this moment that I went head over heels on a molehill that turned out to be surprisingly soft or hollow, or perhaps a combination of both. Rob had gone ahead of me, so he didn't get to witness my pathetic dive into the mud, though he obviously heard the kerfuffle and turned around just as I was dragging myself up, covered in mud and with grass somehow inexplicably in my hair. I thought it was bad form for a mole to pick on someone who is a bit of a kindred spirit, as like moles are said to have quite poor eyesight, mine too is definitely not as good as it used to be. In fact, this had just been demonstrated by the fact that I failed to see a rather large bloody molehill. Rob laughed at me, but I told him that I hadn't fallen down but that the floor had needed a hug. He replied that after millions of years, I was kind of a disappointment and that I was unfit and should try to keep up. I told him that I was fit and that, in fact, I was as swift as a gazelle. He agreed, saying that yes, I was indeed as swift as a gazelle, but one that had been run over by a Land Rover. Eight days ago. Twice.

I was in good company with my fall here, as the humble mole has actually changed the course of English history by murdering one of our kings, but I told Rob he would have to wait until we got to Hull to find out who, how and why.

Anyway, don't get me wrong, I personally like moles and think they look rather cute. Their historical name is also quite pleasing to the ear, as many years ago you would have called a mole a *mouldywarp*, or even an *umpty-tumpt*, which you have got to admit, are both pretty cool names.

Its fur was once highly prized, too, and would have adorned the inside of many a top hat, but only for the richest among us, as moleskins are obviously rather small. To get around this, several of them would have been sewn together and then dyed, as it was practically impossible to find enough pelts of exactly the same colour. I am also reliably informed that they make excellent inner linings for gloves, and they have long been associated with the fronts of waistcoats.

Don't think about eating one, though. William Buckland, who, if you remember, we last met when we were discussing coprolites, famously claimed to have eaten his way through the animal kingdom – a practice known as zoophagy – but when it came to the humble mole, he wasn't a fan. In fact, he considered mole to be possibly the worst thing he had ever tasted, which really quite saying something, and he compared its taste to that of a bluebottle fly, which is pretty disgusting when you think about it, especially when you also consider that Buckland's favourite go-to snack was mouse on toast.

If, for whatever reason, you fancied a pair of trousers made from moles, you would have to find, catch and kill around 500 of the little blighters. It would be worth it, though, as their fur has been compared to velvet, only better. It is very short and dense, and the leather is very soft and supple, but what makes mole fur truly special is the nap, which is the raised fuzzy surface of the fur itself.

Other furry animals tend to have their fur growing towards the tail. Think of a cat, for instance, and stroke it the wrong way, and apart from really annoying the cat, it just doesn't feel right, does it? In fact, this is where the expression *to rub someone the wrong way* comes from. Now, if you grab a mole and stroke that instead, apart from probably getting bitten, you will find that it feels the same whichever way you rub it. Why is this, I hear you ask? Well, it is an evolved feature that helps the mole to reverse quickly in tunnels whenever something hungry with big teeth comes along and tries to eat it. You learn something every day, don't you?

I hobbled along, ignoring the intense pain at the back of my ankle, and decided to just walk it off. We passed through a gate, which told us that many species of birds could be found on the common, including lapwing, snipe and curlew. To old William Buckland, of course, this would have basically been a menu, although, in fairness, there wasn't anything on the sign actually prohibiting you from eating them.

This straight path continued for another few hundred yards, and I had suggested to Rob that we stop for lunch when we arrived at the road, as there was a fishing pond marked on the map and there might be a bench. In fact, just before we got to the road, we saw a picnic bench sitting mysteriously in the middle of a field to our left, so we headed for that instead.

Rob sat down, so I sat down right next to him, which made him give me a funny look. I think he wondered why I wasn't sitting on the other side of it and facing him rather than huddled up next to him as I was, so I had to explain to him that if I did so, I would have the wind in my face. If I sat next to him, the wind would be on my back instead, which would be much more comfortable. I don't think he was convinced, and I am pretty sure he checked his pockets and his bag in case I had stolen anything.

We ate our lunch in silence. The sun was still out, but because the wind had picked up, there was a definite chill in the air. It is amazing how quickly your body cools when you stop walking, and in less than ten minutes, we had finished our sandwiches, drunk our coffee, and we were ready to go again.

Rob magicked a couple of pieces of flapjack out of his pocket, and for one awful moment, I thought he was going to eat both of them. When he instead offered one to me, I accepted it gratefully and reckoned I wouldn't have to murder him in the woods after all.

We re-joined the path and continued heading towards the road, with a small but dark conifer forest on our right. We appeared to be on some kind of campsite, though because it was still the middle of winter, it was totally deserted.

However, there was a dartboard nailed to a tree, which was both a bit random and highly entertaining. Unfortunately, I tend not to take my darts with me when I go walking, mainly because I'm not a psychopath, so we couldn't stop for a game, but we did stop and take a couple of silly photos.

A quick check of the map told us we should head east at the road, which we did, and we hugged the edge as best as we could as there was no path. Most of the traffic slowed down and gave us a wide berth as they passed. Perhaps they were slowing so they could get a look at the two weirdos in the middle of nowhere, I wondered. One or two, however, failed to either slow their vehicles or move across the road, and at least one specifically tried to exterminate us, though luckily, the gods were with us today, and they failed in their evil plan.

Both Rob and I practised various combinations of hand signals involving one or more fingers at the passing miscreants, though I'm not sure they would have seen us as I don't think they were looking, judging by how close they came to us. I often wonder how I am going to die, but being a stain across a piece of tarmac in the middle of winter is certainly not at the top of my list, I can tell you that.

We passed a farm and another golf course, though this one seemed deserted, and after a mile or two, we left the road and joined a small path heading towards Hagg Wood, which we could see off in the distance ahead of us.

It was here that Rob noticed a postcard on the floor, and being as I am the shorter of the two of us, he pointed out that technically I was closer to it, so I should pick it up. You can't argue with logic like that, I thought, as I reached down and discovered it was an antique postcard depicting a busy Edwardian street scene in, of all places, Bradford.

Don't get me wrong, I have nothing against Bradford, and in fact, the scene in the picture looked pretty nice. In fact, it was probably nicer then than it is now, but so many places probably were when you think about it.

It was the randomness of the find that threw us, and neither of us could predict a chain of events that would see such a postcard finding itself out here, in the middle of the countryside, so far from home if you know what I mean.

We toyed with a couple of ideas of what to do with it and considered posting it to someone, perhaps pretending to be a time traveller, but instead, we decided to stick it in the crack of a fingerpost sign of one of the many public footpaths around here. It was a windy day, but Rob managed to get it wedged in nicely, and when we were satisfied that it wasn't going anywhere anytime soon, we moved on. Anyone would think we were six.

We passed one farm, which seemed a hive of inactivity today, and followed the track to the next, which actually turned out to be a collection of very nice houses and converted barns and not a farm at all. We were heading for some woods around a mile away, and as we were so exposed, the wind blew around us fiercely, and I noticed it was starting to get a bit chilly.

Despite the cold, it must be nice to live out here, I thought, with commanding views all around, confident in the knowledge that nobody was going to knock on your door and try to sell you Tupperware or convert you to a new religion or a whole host of other things that you neither want nor need. Indeed, I even have one of those stickers on my door, which basically tells people to go away but which everyone ignores, so every time I answer my door to one salesperson or another, the first thing I ask them is whether or not they can read. My wife thinks I am very rude, and despite my protestation that I am merely interested in the education of others as well as the socio-economic impacts of the dumbing down of society as a whole, she still thinks I can be a bit of a prick at times. She's probably right, but it can also be fun. For instance, the next time you get one of those calls from an unknown number, just pick it up and say, *'It's done, but there's tons of blood everywhere,'* then hang up. You're welcome.

We arrived at the wood, in front of which was a rather large shed, possibly housing chickens or sheep, but probably not moles, although there was no real way to tell for sure. The path led us along a track next to the wood, which we continued along while we talked, but then Rob suddenly stopped dead and pointed slightly to our left.

A huge herd of deer stood in the field adjacent to us, and there were dozens of them, all merrily munching on whatever the farmer had just foolishly planted, but the best bit was that they had not noticed us. Deer are usually such fleeting and nervous animals, especially when it comes to people, so it was a treat to be so close to so many of them all at once. We just stopped and stared, not daring to move, enjoying the view and soaking it all in.

I'm not an expert when it comes to what breed a deer might be, but I was pretty sure that these were roe deer, judging by the fact that most of them had a prominent white rump and no tail. William Buckland would be salivating and firing up the barbecue had he been with us, I imagined, and I also imagined that deer tasted much better than mole, though I can't recall ever having had either. I have tried kangaroo and goat, and I think I even had an emu burger once, but it puzzled me why we don't eat more deer, as they are incredibly common and are considered a pest by some.

One recent study stated there are an incredible 40,000 car accidents every year involving deer, probably because none of them have driving licences. These animals also cause several millions of pounds worth of damage to crops. On top of that, they also target young trees as they find the bark especially appealing due to its flavour and tenderness, and this is at a time when we are trying to plant more trees for environmental reasons. Basically, the deer population is out of balance, or to put it in layman's terms, deer are jerks. I mean, if you saw some adolescent youth wandering around making cars crash, trampling farmers' fields and ripping saplings out of the ground, what would you do? You'd be digging a hole and putting them in it, I reckon. Maybe William Buckland is right, and perhaps we should eat them?

We reluctantly moved on, leaving our new friends behind, who had at least noticed us by now and who seemed to be staring at us en masse, though they made no attempt to flee.

Rob even waved goodbye to them, though they just stared placidly at us, munching on whatever was in their mouths as they did so, and none of them waved back, the jerks.

We joined a narrow lane, and according to the map, we were not far from Wheldrake. I suggested to Rob that we should stop there, as I needed to make use of the facilities, and I think Rob very much enjoyed telling me that I should have gone before I set off. I reminded him that while I would soon be able to relieve myself, he would always be a bonehead, but because he is bigger than me, I did this rather quietly.

Wheldrake slowly came into view, with the most prominent building being something that looked like a water tower. Despite its appearances, with lots of newish-looking houses which were probably from the 1970s, Wheldrake is actually rather ancient. The earliest records state that it belonged to Morcar, Earl of Northumbria, who, if you remember, fought with his brother against King Harald Hardrada back at Fulford. After the events of 1066, and when William the Conqueror took over practically everything, Wheldrake was gifted to a man called William Malet. Not many people have heard of him, but Malet was related to and fought alongside William at the Battle of Hastings, hence his reward.

On top of this, however, Malet was also related to King Harold of England, who, if you also remember, famously took an arrow in the eye during the same battle. It is thought by some people who should well know about these things that it was, in fact, William Malet who took care of King Harold's body after the Battle of Hastings, which would make sense, when you think about it, though we will never really know for sure, of course.

And one last thing about Malet, which is also interesting, is that his mother-in-law was none other than Lady Godiva. She, of course, was famous for another reason. As the story goes, Lady Godiva's husband, Leofric, had inflicted great taxes on the people of Coventry. She appealed to him to lessen their burden, to which he replied he would, but only on one condition. If she rode naked on a horse wearing nothing but her hair, he would reduce the taxes. Lady Godiva thought about this and finally decided that she would and issued a proclamation for the townspeople on the day in question to *'shutt their dores, & clap their windowes downe'*. She kept to her word, mounted her stallion and trotted through Coventry on the back of her nag, but, surprise, surprise, at least one dirty old devil decided not to shut his door and clap his windows down but instead decided to have a peep. This filthy old git was called Tom, and if you haven't guessed already, this is said to be where the term *peeping tom* comes from.

We made it to the Wenlock Arms, and while Rob got us both a beer, I went off to do what I had to do.

We soon found a nice quiet corner, and although there was a handful of people in the pub, it was a fairly relaxing place to be, especially after walking several miles. I sank into a small leather settee, which was quite well worn, but this only worked to make it even comfier, and I could quite happily have stayed here.

Apart from us two, then, there was a solitary man at the bar, who had apparently worked his way through several pints of beer, as well as the barmaid and a group of about half a dozen older ladies at the other end of the room. They were clearly plotting something, as one of them had a pen and paper, and when I finally managed to hear a snippet of their conversation, I was astounded to find out that they were planning a Christmas party, even though Christmas was over ten months away.

Maybe it's a woman thing, and they are more organised, but us men tend not to plan. My thinking on this is that if you don't plan, then you can never be disappointed, as it's not as if your plans can be scuppered. My wife, on the other hand, is always very organised, and I often wonder if she is perhaps ex-military, as she is also pretty scary.

The pub itself was nice enough, with low beamed ceilings and nice warm radiators, but unfortunately, we could not stay long. We still had a few miles to go, so after enjoying our single solitary pint, we were soon back on the road, but not before Rob made use of the facilities. While he was gone, I went to talk to the barmaid and the drunk propping up the bar.

I asked the barmaid if she was local, and she said she was from Heslington, which was where she was currently attending university, and which we had passed through on the way here. I asked her if she knew any good stories about the place, and she said there was one about a pickled brain, but she couldn't remember the details, so it was only later when I got home that I was able to find out all about it, and it was interesting indeed.

The brain, while it was not quite pickled, was found in a bog in 2008. This wasn't the result of a particularly lively student night out and its subsequent discovery in a toilet, but the bog in question was actually a peat bog. Furthermore, the brain was found in the skull that it had occupied while living, although where the rest of this person had gone was and remains an absolute mystery.

This brain, being around 2,000 years old, is actually the best-preserved brain found in Europe, according to the people that should know about these things, although why it is in such good condition is a bit of a mystery. Somewhat alarmingly, perhaps, boffins decided to bury severed pig heads around the area where the brain was found so they could study them for any signs of decomposition and some clues as to what is, or more accurately, what isn't going on. They gave each head a name, too, and one of them was called Napoleon.

I just hope they remember where they put them all. If not, there will be some rather puzzled archaeologists scratching their chins and coming up with all sorts of sacrificial theories in a couple of millennia and possibly thinking that us Yorkshire folk were all a bit barmy, which of course we are.

And lastly, neuroscientists are even working on the preservation of this and other brains, which is called crypto preservation, on the basis that in a few years, we might be able to read them as easily as popping a memory stick into your computer. Wouldn't that be interesting?

The drunken man never said anything, but he did wobble a bit, but after Rob returned and we made to leave, he gave us a smile and a wave and then fell over.

Wheldrake is not a big place, and after a quick look in the church, we were soon back in the fields and heading towards Sutton-upon-Derwent, our finishing point for the day. Our next point of reference was Cheesecake Farm, which sounded very nice, although we couldn't see it as it appeared to be hidden by a small wood.

Walking slowly through some muddy fields, we finally arrived at the wood after getting slightly lost, which was quite frankly somewhat embarrassing considering we were in open countryside with fine views in every direction, and there was even a sign which we had apparently missed. I can only assume that someone had momentarily removed the rather large wooden sign with *public footpath* written on it, then made both themselves and the sign temporarily invisible due to the fact that there was nowhere to hide, waited for us to pass, and then plonked it back in the ground in exactly the same position as before, but there you go. Some people simply have too much time on their hands.

Anyway, Cheesecake Farm was nothing like it had sounded, and there was certainly nothing to suggest cakes or cheese, so we plodded on through increasingly muddy fields. I'm not sure why, but it always seems to be the case that the nearer you get to finishing a walk, the muddier the path gets. This had been the case on almost every stage of our last walk, the Herriot Way, and it was certainly the case today. I knew this was so because my feet now weighed about half a ton, and I was struggling to lift them.

There was nobody along this final stretch of path, which was good, as it meant there were no witnesses when the both of us went slipping and sliding on possibly the muddiest field that has ever existed anywhere in the known universe. It was up to our ankles at some points, and some of it had even managed to work its way into my socks, although I had no idea how.

It was with great relief, then, when we emerged into the pretty little village of Elvington, which appeared to be, perhaps not surprisingly, a victim of recent flooding. Some kind of generator and what was presumably a water pump greeted us on a narrow lane near the church, and various pipes were dotted around here and there, and everything was covered in a thick layer of mud.

We headed to the church, Holy Trinity, more for a sit down than anything else, and immediately noticed a strange object within the grounds. I later found out that it was a lampstand that stood atop some stones recycled from an old font base. I won't tell you how much time I wasted trying to get to the bottom of that one, but I will say that I needed a shave by the time I had finished. And while the church is very nice, there is much more to say about Elvington.

For instance, just a few yards away and over the fields is one of the longest runways in Europe. This is at the former RAF Elvington, a Second World War era airfield that now houses the Yorkshire Air Museum. Although we're not going today, I did visit the place a few years ago, and it is well worth popping in.

The airfield was originally one of the bases used by Number 4 Group RAF, which, if you remember, was based at Heslington Hall. I bet that they didn't have to walk here every time they came, though.

Anyway, after the war, the Americans got hold of the base, which explains why the runway is so long, being over 10,000 feet in length, which is almost two miles. The runway was so long because our transatlantic cousins wanted to use Elvington as a dispersal field for something called Strategic Air Command, which meant that this base would have been used in the event of a nuclear war, presumably also making it something of a target itself. However, almost as soon as they had finished building the runway, it became obsolete, largely because long-range missiles were taking over from dropping bombs out of planes.

Although the base technically stayed in the ownership of the military until the early 1990s, people started using the runway as a racetrack as early as the 1960s. Although it has long been well known within the racing world, Elvington hit the headlines worldwide in 2006 when Top Gear presenter Richard Hammond was involved in a rather bad accident there.

He had been driving a jet-powered dragster called *Vampire* and had been trundling along at almost 320 miles per hour at the time of the crash. This had actually been his seventh run in the vehicle, which was also supposed to have been his final run and was conducted just so the crew could get a little more footage.

What happened has been well studied, and it appears that the front-right tyre of the dragster suffered a blow-out. The car flipped and eventually came to a stop deeply embedded in the grass. Hammond was seriously injured and spent months recovering, and when Top Gear came back on air the following year, this crash was the first thing they showed.

This wasn't the only crash at Elvington, either. Zef Eisenberg, a mixture of television presenter, businessman and daredevil, crashed his own jet-powered vehicle here a decade after Hammond in 2016. His was a motorbike, and he had been attempting the land speed record. According to Eisenberg himself, he did not see the finish line and just kept on going, crashing off the end of the runway at around 230 miles per hour. Despite suffering eleven broken bones, he made a full recovery and was back at Elvington exactly a year after the crash riding the same bike, which had obviously been rebuilt. It is said that he was the country's fastest motorbike crash survivor. Unfortunately, his luck finally ran out right here at Elvington in 2020, when he was killed in a crash while attempting to break the British land speed record in a Porsche 911.

Not all speed attempts end badly at Elvington, though. Records for the fastest wheelie bin and fastest wheelchair were also set here recently, and in a nod to my home city of Hull, I can reveal that the wheelchair belonged to a man called Jason Liversidge, who lives just outside the city and whose van can often be seen zooming around the place.

There are also one or two other little interesting stories to tell about Elvington, with the first one relating to the Second World War. On the night of the 3rd of March 1945, the historical record will tell you that a German aeroplane, a Junkers Ju88 fighter bomber, crashed here, making it the last enemy aircraft to crash land on British soil. There is only one problem with this, as this is far from the full story and is not quite the truth.

Earlier that night, hundreds of Allied bombers had taken off from Elvington and several other bases in the region and had headed off to Germany to bomb an oil refinery as well as a canal crucial for shipping the oil to its destination.

While the Germans had figured out that the allies now had air superiority over most of Europe, they devised a cunning plan called Operation Gisela that would intercept allied aircraft at their most vulnerable point, just as they were about to land at their home bases.

To this end, around 200 German aircraft had also taken off that night, intending to intercept the bombers at the end of their mission. One of these aircraft was the one that ultimately came down here, piloted by an experienced airman, a man called Johann Dreher. Dreher had spent hundreds of hours in the air and had taken part in 400 ground attacks, which is the first thing to suggest that the official account of him hitting trees after misjudging his distance from the ground didn't quite add up. On top of this, he had even been awarded a Knight's Cross, which was the highest award in the German military in the Second World War, so a misjudgement seemed even less likely.

This is where Corporal George Wetherill

comes into the story. He, along with three of his colleagues, had been on duty at Elvington that night, and although he never spoke of this incident, his daughter Sheila discovered a certificate after his death. It turned out that Wetherill had been mentioned in dispatches for shooting down a German aircraft at Elvington that same night, which could only possibly be the one flown by Dreher. Furthermore, Wetherill never mentioned it because of the immense guilt he felt. As well as Dreher and his crew, three people in Dunnington Lodge, a nearby farmhouse, were also killed. These were Richard and Helen Moll and their daughter-in-law, Violet, though their son Richard managed to escape, grabbing his 3-year-old son Edgar on the way out. George Wetherill knew them all personally, hence the immense guilt.

The very last story about this village is actually related to our walk, for, as usual, I have left the best till last. This is perhaps my favourite bit of Elvington's history and concerns a man called Fisher Murray, who is buried in the graveyard here. Rob and I had a walk around looking for it, and it did not take too long at all. The inscription tells us much and reads:

> To the Memory of FISHER MURRAY, A faithful Black Servant, who came from Madeira with Thomas Cheap Esqr. who was Consul there, and after living Sixty Years in

the Family died the 18th Decr. 1821.

There is just one thing wrong with the inscription, and that would be the word *servant*, for Fisher Murray was, in fact, a slave. When I looked at Fisher Murray's burial certificate, it gave his age at the time of his death as 74, meaning he had been living with the Cheap family since he was around 14 years old, which almost exactly coincides with Thomas Cheap's appointment as Consul in Madeira, almost sixty years before in 1763.

We passed by a big old stately home, which perhaps not surprisingly turned out to be Elvington Hall, and I wondered if this had been the home of novelist Hugo Charteris, who definitely lived in the village, although I am not sure where exactly. Charteris grew up in Gloucestershire with his sister Ann, and he may have been introduced to the literary world by James Barrie, better known as J.M. Barrie, creator of Peter Pan. Ann went on to have a rather interesting life, too. Her third husband was Ian Fleming, who, of course, went on to make an absolute fortune from his fictional spy James Bond, and she maybe took his writings a bit too much to heart, as she had affairs with prominent politicians Hugh Gaitskell and Roy Jenkins.

It turns out that Charteris had not lived at the hall after all, but I only found this out long after we had done this walk. He had actually lived at

The Grange, which we had walked past on the way into the village, although it is now called Manor Farm.

Because we had come out at the hall, we must have taken a wrong turn, as our path should have taken us along the river, but it didn't really matter as we had only come a few yards out of our way, and anyway, it had been worth it to see the house. I had seen an old photograph of the hall, which showed it had once been much smaller than it was today.

It was extended at some point in the 1800s by a man called John Carr, who was not someone I had heard of until I walked the Herriot Way with Rob a few months back. We had also taken my dog, Belle, and while we had been doing that walk, we kept coming across Carr, or more accurately, his work, as it was he who built most of Yorkshire's bridges, apparently, and a lot more besides. If this house was anything to go by, then he was as good at houses as he was bridges, and seems as his bridges form the backbone of our road network to this very day, that is a true compliment indeed.

We headed along the road towards Sutton-upon-Derwent and were almost finished for the day, as this was where we had said we would stop. We had left our car here and had taken a bus into York this morning and had been incredibly lucky. We had simply presumed we would be able to get a bus from here but had not checked any timetables, and it turns out that the bus only runs on a Thursday. Luckily, today was a Thursday.

A stone bridge took us over the River Derwent, and on our right was an old canal boat lying in a field. We encountered a ruined house just after the boat, and a bend in the road brought us into the village. While we probably could have gone a bit further, neither of us wanted to. Still, all in all, we both agreed that we had thoroughly enjoyed the first day of the Wilberforce Way, although we had learned absolutely nothing about William Wilberforce, but there's always next time.

The Lunatics And The Labradors

Sutton-upon-Derwent to Pocklington

I had picked Rob up this morning, the plan being to park in Pocklington and get the bus to Wilberfoss and then walk back to Sutton-upon-Derwent to continue our walk.

We nearly never made it, as when I pulled up at Rob's house, I had a little issue. Basically, I had just had my brakes fixed at the garage, but it was only when I tried to stop outside Rob's that I realised they still didn't work, but they had made my horn louder.

The day had already turned bad. First of all, I forgot to go to the gym. That's seven years in a row now. On top of that, my washing machine had stopped pumping out water. But more importantly, I couldn't find my hamster.

All of this was a shame, as it had started so nice when I had woken up to a cuddle from my wife. I can honestly say that there is no finer way to start a day than waking up in the loving embrace of another human being. Unless you're in prison, of course. On a serious note, I'm very happy that I'm with my wife, as my life might well have gone in a different direction on several occasions.

When I was younger and before I met my wife, I had once thought I had met the girl of my dreams. She almost clinched it when she told me she worked with animals until I found out that she was a butcher.

I dumped her in our local McDonalds. Think about it. If you need to break up with somebody, then McDonalds really is the best place to do it. There are no plates or glasses to be broken over your head, no sharp knives or spiky forks to stab you in the heart with, and on top of that, if things really go south, you can always hide behind a fat kid.

Anyway, we parked the car and went to find the bus station, which was not so much a station, but more of a solitary piece of metal with a sign stuck on it. We waited patiently and felt almost special when our bus actually turned up on time.

While we had been patiently waiting, lots of other people had also turned up, most of them probably bound for York. Perhaps not surprisingly, most of them were in the older age bracket, and many of them had accessories such as walking sticks and zimmer frames and false legs and the like. What was surprising was the way they all turned into vicious animals when the bus pulled up and opened its doors. Rob and I stood there as they swarmed around us and charged the bus, scanning their passes as they inundated the driver with an impressive stampede somewhat reminiscent of the wild-west. I've noticed that old people are not just like this at bus stops, either. Let's just say that the true nature of a human being clearly shows when the supermarket opens a second till.

Many of them went upstairs, even those with walking sticks and zimmer frames and even the one-legged man, which was really surprising, so we had to make do with a couple of meagre seats on the bottom and towards the back. Unfortunately, these faced the wrong way, which was not good for people like me who get travel sickness, which worried Rob at least a little. A young woman sat opposite us, whom I discreetly pointed out to Rob, as she either had two really ugly children or two seriously cool Pokémon. Regarding the old people again, my own great-grandfather came back from the war with one leg, though we never did find out who it belonged to.

Yet more pensioners boarded the bus, and I almost gave up my seat for one of them, though I didn't really want to. Luckily, they must have come from Lourdes or perhaps the Vatican, but anyway, some kind of miracle was performed as they somehow lifted their zimmer frame and stowed it at the top of the luggage rack and then hopped off upstairs to join the rest of the blue rinse brigade. Still, the fleeting feeling of guilt reminded me of that moment when you're laying the table, and you notice that one fork isn't actually all that clean, so you have to quickly decide which family member you like the least.

Talking of food, I must confess that we had stopped at a rather famous fast-food restaurant on the way here today. When Rob had asked me what I wanted, I told him I wanted a beef salad. He looked puzzled, so I explained that if vegetarians are allowed to call their creation a soy sausage, I can call my burger a beef salad. Furthermore, I briefly ranted, I haven't fought my way to the top of the food chain just to become a vegetarian. Anyway, as I stuffed my face, I gave thanks for the fact that we live in modern times and I don't have to hunt burgers myself. I had a coffee as well, but then I had to. Before my first cup of coffee, I hate everybody. That doesn't necessarily change after I've had that coffee, but it does feel much better.

We eventually jumped off the bus and made

our way towards Sutton on Derwent, and just past Wilberfoss, a shallow hill soon allowed the views to open up all around us, although the road was busier than expected for such an early hour. Most of the passing vehicles moved a few millimetres away from the kerb so as not to kill us, but only just. There was, however, one single, smoky old truck that tried to squash the pair of us and make us one with the tarmac, and he probably would have managed it had we not squeezed out of the way a millisecond before impact. It was lucky I brought my fingers, I thought, as I stuck two of them up in the air.

As we walked along, we discussed important issues such as can dragons blow out candles (no chance) as well as how do hedgehogs have sex (carefully). We talked about various odd people we had met recently and came to the conclusion that there are people who are living proof that total brain failure does not always lead to physical death, and we also made a list of things that look good in leopard skin, which basically amounted to leopards and not much else, and certainly did not include human beings of any shape or size.

We shared odd snippets of information with each other, such as the fact that psychologists have discovered that for human beings to maintain good mental health, we should hug approximately nine people every day. An alternative is to punch one key person in the face. Really hard.

We also tackled some of the great philosophical issues of our time, such as why are snorers always the first ones to fall asleep, though I told Rob that he was probably a bit clueless on this one, as he was always the first one to fall asleep. And we asked why was it that we might be really good at stuff until, that is, somebody watches you doing that stuff? Strange but true, we agreed.

I could see a village ahead of us, just visible through the trees. The visibility was great today; in fact, it was a bit too great, and a gleaming low sun hung in an almost cloudless sky, partially blinding us. I laughed out loud, which probably made Rob a bit uncomfortable, as I thought to myself how I am never happy with the weather, although, in all honesty, today was a perfect day for us to continue our walk.

I had remembered to put some sun cream on today and toyed with the idea of putting my hat on, which languished somewhere at the bottom of my rucksack. But the truth was that I couldn't be bothered, as to do so, I would have to stop walking, take it off my back and rummage through it. Rob said I was rather idle, and he would be right, and in fact, it is a good thing that breathing is a reflex. In fact, when one of my teachers asked me to characterize myself in five words, I replied, '*quite lazy*'.

Beside me, Rob's bald head glimmered in the sunshine, and I imagined that somewhere in this low and wide valley, in one direction or another, someone was currently being blinded by the flash of sunlight that was inevitably bouncing off his big shiny noggin.

We made our way along the road, still dodging the early morning commuters who were all apparently convinced that they were in the qualifying stage of the Monte Carlo Rally, and we soon discovered the source of all of this traffic. A recycling plant stood to our left, quite unexpectedly in the middle of nowhere, and there had presumably been a shift change, with lots of staff coming and going. I think most of them had learned to drive in Mogadishu, either that, or they had not learned to drive at all.

Luckily, just after this, the road quietened somewhat. Presumably, this was because most of the traffic had either crashed or headed north to the main road, and not south, where we were headed.

We were alongside the village of Norton-upon-Derwent now, and I had suggested to Rob that we skip the village for two reasons. One was because it wasn't even on our itinerary, and the other was because the village was a liar.

Allow me to explain. When you hear that a

place is called Norton-upon-Derwent, you expect
first of all that it is called Norton, which indeed it
was. However, it might be reasonable to suppose
that it stood on the River Derwent, hence the
name, but this was simply not so. The river
is actually around a mile to our east, which
therefore makes it a liar, and which meant that
there was nothing to see there.

Anyway, most of the action seemed to be
here, as a recycling truck had just pulled up in
front of us, and we witnessed a crack team of
Britain's most eager refuse operatives emptying
the bins of Norton-not-upon-Derwent with all
of the excitement of a snuggle of sloths. If they
had been going any slower, they would have gone
back in time.

We passed them by, only to have them pull
their truck in front of us once again a few yards
further up the road at the next house, and I
jokingly said to one of them that they could have
given us a lift. He smiled and said that yes, they
could have, although we would have had to work
for our lift, though when I thought about it, I was
not sure I could move at a slow enough speed to
fit in with them.

Luckily, we left them behind when a
large farm vehicle which vaguely resembled a
combine harvester came zooming from the
other direction, filling up both sides of the road
and making passage for anything other than an

anorexic stick insect more or less impossible. As I glanced over my shoulder, I saw one puzzled farmer and half a dozen bin men slowly scratching their heads, and when I say slowly, I really do mean it in the deepest sense of the word.

As I said, we really couldn't have picked a better day. The sun gods were shining all around us, and the first signs of spring were beginning to announce themselves. Snowdrops were beginning to flower beneath the hedges to our right, along with a few other plants that I could not name. However, there had clearly been a lot of rain, as most of the ditch was full to the top with muddy brown water.

There was a certain amount of heat in the sunshine today, which made me glad I had put that sun cream on this morning. As we made our way slowly along the twisting and turning road, cars occasionally flew past, once again at great speed, and some of them were even using all four wheels. We both agreed that we would be happy when we were off this road, and the only good thing about it was the very nice houses which dotted its length. I made a mental note to buy one when my big lottery win came in.

Norton-not-upon-Derwent wasn't a particularly big village, though it did seem rather long, and we walked alongside it for what seemed to be an age. Eventually, however, we knew we had reached the other end of it, as a road sign pointed to our right and to its southern end.

Just next to this junction, we found a spooky old abandoned house and being the childish imps that we are, we just couldn't resist a quick look around it. A lane ran down the right-hand side of it, which we followed for a few feet before cutting through some prickly bushes and into the garden. We did get a bit mauled by a rather nasty holly bush and some kind of hawthorn, and there might even have been the odd cactus in there, judging by the scrape I felt across my forehead. I didn't see anything, though, as I had my eyes shut, but I must add that Rob fared far worse than me. This was because he was much taller, of course, and it was, therefore, his own fault, so he deserves no sympathy from anyone, I told him.

Inside the house, crumbling plaster walls and rotten wooden joists threatened to kill us at any moment, but I wasn't worried. What with technology being what it is nowadays, if the worst did happen, the respective authorities would no doubt find our cold and crushed corpses by tea time at the latest, due to all the devices people carry around with them.

We even made our way upstairs, and surprisingly the staircase never collapsed at all, despite the rather substantial weight placed upon it by two lazy old chubbies. While we're on this subject, my muscles are, in fact, underneath my rather substantial belly. In fact, I love my rock-hard, honed six-pack so much, I merely protect it with a good layer of lard, I told Rob.

Rob had to duck as he went through the doors, as this house had been built for an older generation, who were clearly vertically challenged, to say the least.

Upstairs, we found rooms still adorned with wallpaper and in surprisingly good condition considering the house did not have windows as such, but just holes in the wall, thus allowing nature to enter at will. I half expected to find a family of owls living up there, but we found nothing.

However, in the last room we went in, which I would call the front bedroom, we did find something quite surprising. Someone had been sleeping in there pretty recently, it seemed, as there was a quilt and some pillows leaning up against the wall. This made me feel a bit uneasy, and I suddenly felt as if I had eyes on me, which was silly as there was no one around, but anyway, I told Rob I was nothing but a chicken and that I was off, and although he laughed, he was pretty quick to follow me.

A sign told us it was still two miles to Sutton-upon-Derwent, which actually was on the

Derwent, of course, not like its more northerly neighbour. I suggested to Rob that we had better get a move on, as technically we had not yet even resumed our walk, even though we had been walking for almost an hour, and he agreed, so off we went.

The weather changed a bit, but unfortunately, this was not for the better, but then how could it have been, as it had been such a nice day anyway. Clouds began to block the sun, and the wind picked up considerably, and it was blowing straight in our faces.

In the distance, we thought we could see the first signs of Sutton-upon-Derwent behind the trees, but on reflection, it was simply more trees, so unless the people of the village lived in treehouses, we still had a fair way to go.

As well as having a long way to go, one more of those giant tractors came along, causing us another problem by forcing us to jump in a ditch and have a quick swim, but rather luckily, the water only came up to our necks. Well, actually, it came up to my neck, but only as far as Rob's knees. Dragging ourselves out through a patch of nettles, I suggested to Rob that this was still better than being dead, but he didn't see the funny side.

Thankfully, the tractor only left the road moderately covered in manure, so we could at least pick our way along it, and we soon passed a dog kennel that was also a pig farm and a cattery, so it was probably not one of the quietest places to be early in the morning.

A gang of cyclists suddenly appeared on the road ahead of us, and although I did not know what the collective term for those who choose to ride around on two wheels actually is, I would expect it is a mob or a posse of cyclists, or something very similar. Actually, it turned out to be a *banana* of cyclists. They were all clad in the brightest yellow, you see, and I suspect this was not in any way related to reasons of fashion or style.

They passed us by, almost at warp speed, and as we turned around and watched them disappear behind us, they hit the booby traps left by the tractor, and let's just say they were no longer yellow.

Quite unexpectedly, the road stopped here, or more accurately, we came to a junction and had to choose left or right. Left would take us east, which was the general direction we wanted to be going in, but a quick check of the map told us to go right, or west, which was counter-intuitive but was, in fact, the correct way.

It could not be far to the village now, I suggested to Rob, and he almost guffawed out loud, which suggested that he had little faith in my navigation skills. We plodded on, however, and after briefly being threatened by another bunch of renegade cyclists, clad in an even brighter shade of yellow that was probably radioactive, such was the pain to our eyes, we also encountered a family of four, intent upon a muddy walk through the fields. The parents looked happy, clearly thinking of the pain they were about to inflict upon their beloved offspring by removing them from society and their various electronic devices for the next couple of hours. The children also looked thrilled, but in a manner which perhaps suggested they would rather have sticks poked in their eyes while having their feet set on fire, which, when you think about it, would at least mean they would not have to go for their stupid bloody walk.

We were finally in the village, which meant we had the safety of actual paths to walk on and would no longer have to take our chances with farm traffic, demented sportaholics and rally drivers, I suggested to Rob. This was not to be, he replied, nodding ahead.

A succession of middle-aged female joggers was heading in our direction, which formed a large group that, for some reason, I had not quite noticed. This was probably because the shade of yellow that they had all chosen to wear was one or two lumens less offensive than what I had become accustomed to seeing already today. My eyes, therefore, had failed to adjust to the new lighting conditions, and it was this that rendered these recycled teenagers more or less invisible to my eyes. I said to Rob that it is no coincidence that yellow also means cowardly. I think he rolled his eyes but tried not to let me see, the coward.

I'm not sure why they were jogging, to be honest. They were doing all the motions that joggers tend to do, such as alternately swinging their arms slightly higher than they would when they walked and lifting their knees just a touch as joggers also tend to do, but despite all of this, and despite being in the correct uniform, which must be compulsory around here, they were going at about the same speed that Rob and myself had been doing all morning.

Nonetheless, they could still do us considerable damage if they chose to trample us. Death by a thousand cuts is just as much a death as being squashed by a world record breaking pumpkin, so we stood aside and allowed them to pass, giving each and every one of them a cheery *morning* greeting. Notice that I missed out the *good* from before the *morning*. There is nothing good about being blinded or trampled by old people at this time of the day.

Sutton-upon-Derwent seemed to be just as long a village as Norton-not-upon-Derwent, but at least it had the distinction of actually being on the river. Anyway, we made our way through it, slowly heading south, and encountered many fine houses and several cheery dog walkers, none of whom were wearing offensive shades of yellow.

I did wonder who lived in these large and comfortable looking houses, and I came to the conclusion that it was not poor, struggling writers, no matter how good they were. Rob said that he suspected it was not lifeguards either, for that is his profession, although profession is maybe something of an overstatement, I suggested. With friends like us, who needs enemies, I reminded Rob. The nicest house was the *Old Well House*, or at least that's what I thought, and I decided that I would also buy this one when I won the lottery. The kids could then live in our old one, I chuckled.

We passed the bus stop where we had waited for our bus to York on our previous visit, yet still the village went on, and eventually, after what seemed like a ridiculously long time, we finally reached the other end. For the last few hundred yards, though, someone had been following us, which alarmed me somewhat, though Rob just laughed.

The person in question was dressed, well, there is no other way to say this, but he was dressed like a tramp. His clothes were torn and didn't really fit him, and he was also rather filthy.

Rob suggested that he just wanted to join us, as following our manure incident on the road a while back, he probably thought we were one of his kind. To be honest, it is very important not to judge people by their looks, I reminded Rob. For instance, not every badly unkempt person you see is homeless. It could well be that they simply live with 3 females and only have 1 bathroom.

As we wandered along, Rob asked if it was socially acceptable to ask homeless people if they like house music, and after carefully deliberating the question, I advised him that it was fine, so long as you are bigger than them.

Anyway, luckily, the gentleman in question sat down at a bench which was at the bend in the road that finally marked the end of Sutton-upon-Derwent. We continued on our merry way, and as I glanced around to make sure he wasn't following us, which he wasn't, he did give us both a merry wave, which was really very nice of him, I reckon.

Interestingly, a sign announced that the land around here belonged to Liz. Not getting it? Well, the farm in question was Woodhouse Grange, and this was part of the Crown Estate, so technically, it belonged to the queen.

Unfortunately, however, like so many things in life, it is not that simple. While the estate might technically belong to the queen, it is not actually hers, which I will be the first to admit, does not make much sense. Allow me to explain, or at least try to.

The Crown Estate belongs to the reigning monarch *in right of the crown*, which is to say that it is owned by the monarch, whoever that might be, for the duration of their reign. However, and this is where it gets a bit tricky, it is not the monarch's private property, which means it cannot be sold on, and the revenues from the estate do not belong to the monarch, which again begs the question, *what is the bloody point?*

Well, let's be honest, if it was run by the government, the Crown Estate would probably have gone bust or been sold off many years ago. Instead, it is run by a board and manages to turn a tidy profit amounting to hundreds of millions of pounds per year. This profit is paid directly to the treasury, which spends it on such important necessities as things that go bang and having parties in Downing Street, but crucially, it is also the amount of profit made that decides how much cash the queen gets every year.

This arrangement used to be called the civil list, which previously set a cash amount to be paid to senior and some not-so-senior royals every year. This list had long been kept secret, but when details were finally released to the public for the first time in 2002, it revealed some interesting details.

First of all, it showed that almost three-quarters of the money paid via the civil list was used for staff salaries, while around £100,000 was spent on booze. Almost £20,000 went on vet's bills, presumably to look after Queenie's beloved Corgis, and her electricity bill was around a third of a million pounds, which is about the average price we will all be paying pretty soon, I imagine. And surprisingly, Liz also received a rather large water and sewerage bill that year, as it turned out that Windsor Castle had a dodgy water meter which had been under-estimating her usage for a number of years. Yes, even the queen has to go to the toilet.

Anyway, the civil list is long gone, replaced by something called the Sovereign Grant in 2012. This simplified the process and basically said that whatever amount of profit the Crown Estate pays to the treasury, a fixed percentage will be paid back to the queen. Initially, this was set at 15%, which certainly gave the queen a good chunk of cash, but in 2017, this went up to 25%, basically because they realised Buckingham Palace would pretty much soon fall down unless they got the builders in more or less straight away.

When I was reading about this, I also came across an article that debunked the idea that the queen also owns all of our coastline. This common fallacy, which I had, in fact, believed for quite a long time, has never really been true. However, much like the seawater around our tiny little island, the story does get a bit murky in places.

It turns out, then, that the queen does own a fair bit of our coastline, around 45% or so, although she only owns the tidal bit, which is the bit that gets wet every day. There is even a map you can look at, which gives you a very clear picture of this. You might imagine, then, that this land is just around the coastline, but you would be wrong. For instance, a quick look at this map told me that Liz owns land just to the west of Sutton-upon-Derwent, at a place called Moreby Hall, just south of Naburn, which is itself just south of the city of York, which the last time I checked, was not a seaside resort or anywhere near the coast at all, really. This is, in fact, a staggering forty miles from the sea, and she would have owned even more if the locals hadn't built a lock there, meaning that the river beyond this point was no longer tidal and therefore not subject to Her Majesty's little laws. Interestingly, much of the River Trent is also owned by the queen, also to a point near a place called Sutton, but obviously, Sutton-on-Trent, which is even further from the sea than Sutton-upon-Derwent.

Luckily, in my home city of Hull, with its long history of being a bit awkward when it came to kings, queens and basically all governments in general, we decided to build our little tidal barrier exactly where the River Hull empties into the Humber, which means she can't get her filthy little mitts on any of it at all.

Moving on and leaving Sutton behind for the last time, we headed east, and as the sun had come back out, we were now being blinded from our right, which at least made a change. The road was straight and long, and I had read that it was of Roman origin, which was not surprising. This allowed the traffic to get to speeds that would almost transport you back in time if you had included the optional flux capacitor when you had bought your car.

Most of the passing traffic was very polite, though, or should I say most of the drivers were, and they would pull a few feet out into the road, thereby merely showering us in a cloud of choking dust, which was probably a mix of asbestos from car brake pads mixed in with a nice bit of pollen to make us both a bit sneezy.

However, one car, presumably driven by someone who generally uses a white stick whenever they are out walking, refused to move at all, which made me wish I had brought my hiking poles today, though sadly, I had not.

I'm not sure what I would have done, but I feel that whenever I have my sticks with me, cars just seem to give you that much more room as they pass. As it was, we were forced to walk on the grass verge instead, which was not at all level, and which was pockmarked with molehills, rabbit holes and other assorted booby traps. You would think the molehills would be fairly solid, but when I inadvertently stood on one while trying not to have my feet or possibly my head crushed under a passing Toyota Corolla, I almost disappeared for good.

We began to notice lots of water in the fields to our right, which was a worry, as, after all, these were fields, as opposed to lakes, which is where you would generally find lots and lots of water. As far as I was aware, we had not had ridiculous amounts of rain lately, but then Rob pointed out that we actually had, and that I was just a bit stupid when it came to remembering things.

In fact, we had recently suffered from a succession of storms, which those lovely weathermen and weatherwomen love to name, and over the past few weeks, we had variously been visited by the likes of Dudley, Eunice and Franklin. I'm not sure which one of these scallywags had destroyed my greenhouse, but I know it was one of them.

Thinking about it, those names are not really appropriate for storms when you think about it. I mean, have you ever met anyone called Dudley, Eunice or Franklin who might seem like they would be the type to have smashed all of your windows, ripped your fence down, and thrown your trampoline into next door's garden? No, of course not. In fact, have you ever met anyone with one of those names at all? Probably never. Surely, then, they should use names such as Wayne, Gazza and Britney?

At the time of writing, by the way, we still have the delights of storms Gladys, Herman and Jack to contend with. Not exactly petrifying, are they? Storm Gladys, seriously?

Anyway, whatever had been this way had dumped a lot of water, well, everywhere.

As we made our way along, Rob said that he could see some traffic lights in the distance, but I saw nothing and could not think why anybody would build traffic lights out here, as the map showed there was nothing but straight roads for the next few miles.

He was right, though, but I told him that even a stopped clock was right twice a day. If you remember, Rob has the advantage of height, and as I am a bit of a shorty, it was a few moments later, when we were somewhat closer, that I finally saw the traffic lights.

They appeared to be controlling traffic on a presumably narrow bridge, and as we got closer, we saw that this was exactly the case. This was Hagg Bridge, which was not exactly the best name for a bridge, but who am I to say?

Anyway, it looked all nice and new, as indeed it was. It had just been re-opened after being more or less rebuilt, something which took a bit longer than expected because the builder that did it used cheap concrete, and some of it had to be taken down and rebuilt yet again.

The problem with the bridge today was not the structure, though; it was what was underneath it. The bridge should cross the Pocklington Canal, which we intended to follow from here all the way to Pocklington, as well as a small beck, but instead of these two watercourses, there was just a continuation of the lake that had started back up the road towards Sutton-upon-Derwent.

As we crossed the bridge, we saw a couple with a dog, and the man was dressed as if he knew the area. That might sound a bit silly, but he was dressed like a gamekeeper, so we went to talk to him.

His name was Markus, and he was indeed some sort of gamekeeper, all clad in tweed with a gamekeeper's hat to top it all off. All he needed was the shotgun, which was probably in his Land Rover that he had just climbed out of moments before, and all in all, I got the distinct impression that he was a bit of a character, but an incredibly nice one.

Unfortunately, he was not local, which made

our hearts sink a little, as the path we had wanted to take was clearly flooded, and the map I had brought along did not cover enough of the area to show us an alternative.

Luckily, however, he knew this area well, as he came up here to shoot, he informed us. As we talked, his wife, or at least we presumed the lady to be his wife, took their dog down to the water, where it promptly turned into a fish and jumped straight in.

The flooded fields had been like this for a week, Markus told us, and would probably take another two weeks to drain, so unless we wanted to set up camp and wait it out for a fortnight, we would have to find an alternative route.

Thankfully, as I had already said, he knew the area well and gave us directions that would get us to the canal. He told us to follow this road to the end, turn left, and then go straight on until we came to a chap who was chopping a tree down. He then told us to turn left at the wood-cutter and follow the track to the end, where we would find the canal, hopefully not as flooded as it was here.

Rob and I looked at each other, and I just felt that I had to query the wood-cutter part of the directions. What if he had finished and gone home, I asked, but Markus was adamant that he would still be there. I also queried the identity of this wood-cutter, and Markus said that he was called Mike. These were perhaps among some of the strangest directions we had ever been given, which basically amounted to *turn left at the axe-man*, but as we had no choice, we said we would give it a try.

Before we left, the lady came back with the dog, which proceeded to shower us all with some of the finest Yorkshire floodwater. I wasn't bothered, as my dog does this all the time, and it meant I wouldn't need a shower later, of course. This dog was similar to Belle, my own dog, and was some kind of labrador cross. They absolutely love water, and Belle has been on one or two long-distance walks with me where she has ended up absolutely drenched, so she would have loved it here today.

We said goodbye and wished them well and moved off, following the road around a couple of bends where we found the left turn that we had been instructed to take. A sign here pointed right to a café and butcher, which made me wonder if this was the same person suffering from some kind of psychosis.

We had another one of our odd and rambling conversations here, and I chuckled as I thought how good it was to have someone you can really talk to, who, no matter what you say, will never think you an idiot. Of course, this is only because we both know that the other one really is an idiot, and we have simply accepted the fact, but that's good enough for me.

Rob started it, advising me that he had found his first grey pubic hair the other day, a sure sign of getting old. He said he had gotten really excited, but not as excited as the other people in the lift, which raised a smile to my lips and made my eyebrows do funny things.

In return, I explained to Rob the shenanigans that I had been up to at the gym I joined recently. Last week, for instance, I broke one of my own records when I managed to hold my belly in for over 90 minutes. On a serious note, I set myself a target last month of losing 10 pounds. Four weeks on, and I only have 15 left to go.

My problem is that I eat too much food. Not that I'm a good cook, though. In fact, whenever I am cooking, we usually pray after our meal rather than before. Also, indigenous peoples have been known to stop by my house asking if they can dip their arrows in my soup.

We wandered on, passing the occasional house every now and then that were dotted along either side of this stretch of the road, most of which seemed to somehow have Rossmoor in their name. Rossmoor House stood next to Rossmore Grange, which was behind Rossmoor Cottage, and there were more besides, but I'm sure you get the point.

Somewhere deep in the woods, someone was having a fire, and the smell was far from unpleasant and reminded me of winter fires we had had while camping a couple of years before. The sun was still shining high in the sky, but it was partly obscured by the trees above us as we followed the road, and after not too long, we began to hear the faint buzz of a chainsaw.

Lo and behold, just a few hundred yards further, we came across a man chopping a tree down, so we immediately went to talk to him. He had a huge trailer attached to his Mitsubishi Man-wagon or whatever type of beast it actually was, on top of which was piled a surprisingly dangerous amount of wood. This guy was a true daredevil, I suspected.

When we got talking, he clearly knew who Markus was, indicated by the knowing nod that he gave when I mentioned his name, which I interpreted to mean that Markus was indeed a bit of a character. We talked about the flooded canal and the recent storms, and he told us that the tree he was chopping up had come down in the ridiculous winds of the previous weekend. He was taking it to his house and intended to eventually use it in his wood burner, and he also gave us a lesson on wood burning. This tree was an oak tree, and he told us that oak is an excellent wood to burn and will help keep your chimney clean, apparently, and it will also burn rather slowly, which is good. Ash is another good wood to burn, and it can actually be burned immediately, although it is still better to allow it to season, and this is also similar to fir, which also smells quite wonderful, his words, not mine.

I could have talked to him all day, but time would not allow it, so we bade him farewell and moved on. Rob mentioned how much you learn simply by stopping and talking to people, and he was right, but it is important to mention that you have to listen, too. That is why we have one tongue and two ears, he added.

The track took us through a gate and past another fine house that would befit a lottery winner, leading us onto a narrow green lane. Brilliant white snowdrops were beginning to poke through the grass beneath the hedge, and it wasn't long before we saw a bridge ahead of us, a sign that we were back at the Pocklington Canal. The signs didn't look promising, however, as behind the bridge, we could see yet more standing water.

Climbing onto the top of the bridge, the surrounding fields were indeed well and truly flooded, but along the side of the canal, the path followed the embankment and was, in fact, above the water level, but only by a few inches.

We discussed walking back to the road and continuing into Melbourne that way but unanimously decided to try the canal path instead, primarily because we were both approximately the same mix of stubborn, reckless and stupid.

This bridge, by the way, was somewhat imaginatively named *Bridge Number Five*, although Rob was probably right when he added that it was at least better than Hagg Bridge, something I found impossible to argue against.

Initially, the going was good, but then we began to encounter the odd puddle, which soon became a torrent and seemed to be where the canal was systematically emptying into the fields to our left.

We passed many such spots, and we were both somewhat concerned about what lay ahead, as we did not want to get a mile or two down the line only to have to turn back and cover this distance again. After briefly considering turning back now, that mix of stubbornness and stupidity won out once more, and we carried on recklessly.

We did get a bit wet and had to climb through the odd prickly bush, which at least gave us a bit of height advantage over the puddles below, and we only lost a small amount of blood, something that a simple standard transfusion would probably fix. Eventually, though, we arrived at Bridge Number Six, which actually turned out to be Swingbridge Number Six, upon closer inspection of the sign.

Although the Wilberforce Way continued along the path in a straight line here, we were taking a small detour into Melbourne, a small village just a few hundred yards to the south, where we fully intended to support the local economy in whichever way we could, though hopefully in the pub.

A muddy lane led us south towards the houses, but we stopped momentarily to inspect a branch that hung precariously in the trees above. It had snapped, presumably in the ferocious winds of the previous storm, and had become lodged in another branch as it had begun to fall, which is where it remained now.

However, the wind had picked up, and the whole thing was dancing in the space above our heads, and it looked as if the branch could release and fall at any minute, possibly resulting in a sub-optimal outcome for us should it fall and hit us on the cranium. After a moment or two of hesitation, Rob continued on, and I immediately followed, confident in the knowledge that any falling object would probably hit the top of Rob's head well before it got down to my level.

A left turn into Melbourne revealed a sleepy, quiet village, though there were some noisy workmen making a bit of a racket while digging up a road. I say workmen because they were all men, and I know you have to be careful nowadays, but there you go.

Some of the houses along the main street had very interesting names. My favourites were Greenacres, Nirvana, and Jackdaw Cottage, though there were lots more. In a similar vein, most of the houses down my street have equally interesting names. For instance, mine is called Seventy-two.

Anyway, we passed the village store, which was closed, and carried on until we came to the local pub, which was the Melbourne Arms. We had a quick rest on the first of the many picnic benches in front of the place, enjoying the warm sunshine on our faces, and then Rob went to try the door.

Alas, it was locked, so we would not be supporting the local economy today, but we did stay and eat our lunch, courtesy of their benches. It was still quiet, and the only person to pass was a dog walker, who didn't stop but did give us a cheery hello, although her dog offered us a bit of a nasty growl that suggested he would be more than happy to remove some of our fixtures and fittings, given the chance.

We got talking about dogs and ended up in an argument over what was better, a cat or a dog. I consider myself a bit of an expert in this field, as

I have examples of both species living within my home, whereas Rob has neither. I'm not saying his opinion doesn't count or that he doesn't know what he's on about, but on this subject, at least, he simply doesn't know what he's on about.

I love all of my animals, but for different reasons, and while it is true that you can train a cat to do anything the cat wants to do at the moment it wants to do it, dogs are on another level altogether. I mean, can you imagine a blind person having a guide cat? Or the police using one to chase down criminals? Perhaps you could use a tiger or a panther or something equally big, but after it had efficiently scalped the juvenile delinquent you had just set it on, and with cats being cats, you know full well that you would probably be next. Still, it would be fun to watch.

Whether you are a dog or a cat person, it is always very hard when they die. We lost our dog, Charlie, a while back, and me and the wife had a game of *rock, paper, scissors* to decide who was going to tell our young son, who was only four at the time. I lost the game, and when it came to breaking the bad news, I tried to do it in terms he would understand. I asked him if he remembered the baby bird we had found on the path the other day, which we had later buried in our garden. I could see the truth slowly sinking in, and a tear began to form in one of his eyes as he asked, *'Charlie fell out of a tree?'*

As part of his lunch, Rob pulled out a banana and promptly devoured it, and I reminded him of an important fact I had read. Apparently, people eat more bananas than monkeys, I duly informed my cretinous friend, to which he replied that he was not at all surprised, as he could not remember the last time he had eaten a monkey. Although this was not quite what I had meant, I had to reluctantly admit that he was technically right.

We discussed Melbourne and decided that there must be something in the water; either that or the sheer proliferation of old airfields around this part of the country just makes people want to drive like lunatics, for just a couple of miles outside of the village is Melbourne Raceway. This racetrack is used chiefly for drag racing, which quite sadly does not involve men dressed as women and running down the straight, but thankfully does involve all sorts of crazy vehicles competing to be the fastest thing on four wheels and sometimes two.

As well as your typical drag racing cars, however, there is also a fair bit of unconventional racing which goes on here, including an unlikely-sounding steam-powered rocket-propelled motorbike, as well as the world's fastest shed. Yes, I said shed. Go figure. Kevin Nicks, presumably a recent escapee from one asylum or another, has managed to engineer a humble garden shed that he drove at speeds of over 100 miles per hour. Perhaps even more bizarrely, the thing is even road legal, which must have been something of a sight when he drove it all the way up here from his home in Oxfordshire.

As we were finishing our lunch, a small child rode up on his bicycle. He leaned it against the fence and asked if the pub was open, and we told him that, sadly, it was not. They start young around here, I mentioned to Rob, as the young man, who clearly chose not to believe us, went over to the door to try it himself. Finding it locked, he then gave it a good knock before peering through one of the windows, which he also banged on.

I told him that there is an off-licence in Pocklington where he could probably get some cider if he was that desperate, but he just laughed and said that he knew the owners, after which he gave up and rode off on his bike the same way he had come from.

We had begun to cool down as we sat there eating our lunch, as you tend to do in winter, of course, so it wasn't long before we were soon off again.

Unfortunately, off, in my case at least, meant walking in the wrong direction, and my good friend Rob just stood still and let me go. I didn't realise he wasn't behind me for at least fifty yards, which annoyingly meant that I had to retrace my steps, adding unnecessary distance to my journey. Once again, with friends like that, who needs enemies?

We followed the track down the side of the pub, which would take us back to the canal, and although this would technically mean we would miss out a few hundred feet of the Wilberforce Way, we weren't doing this walk as purists. Anyway, Melbourne is a nice diversion for anyone doing the route.

Almost as soon as we turned into this lane, we met an elderly gentleman who was out walking his dog, only there was a slight problem, as he had no dog. He was standing in the middle of the track scratching his head and looking towards the canal, with his dog lead in one hand.

We chatted to him and asked him if the path ahead of us was flooded, as it had been further back, but he told us it was fine and he had just been down there with his dog, though he quickly corrected himself and said it was his daughter's dog. He had last seen it near the water, he went on, and it usually followed him at some point, but today it was being awkward. He never actually said awkward, but I cannot bring myself to write the word which spewed from between his lips, so let's just say he was a down to earth sort of guy.

We asked him what type of dog it was and promised to send it his way if we saw it and headed north, on the lookout for a black labrador. Nearing the canal at the other end of the path, we had seen absolutely exactly zero dogs, and as we turned around to look back, we could still see the old man stood just as he had been, holding his empty dog lead and scratching his head.

We stood by the canal, or more accurately, a small marina attached to the canal, where several very pretty canal boats were moored up, presumably for the winter. Several of them looked lived in and sported solar panels and wind turbines, and one even had smoke coming out of its chimney, so there was either someone inside, or it was on fire.

One of them was called New Horizons, and this was a boat I was familiar with, but first, a little about the canal.

The Pocklington Canal connects the River Derwent, not surprisingly and as you might expect, with the small town of Pocklington. It opened in the early 1800s, with the builders starting at the end nearest the river, which meant that sections could be opened as and when they were completed, which makes a lot of sense when you think about it. For years, it prospered and saw all sorts of goods carried up and down its length; however, it eventually passed into the hands of the York and North Midland Railway Company. They obviously focused their attention on the railway lines that they owned and more or less neglected the canal to minimise costs. When the railways were nationalised in 1948, the canal was well and truly stuffed, and it soon fell into severe disrepair.

The whole thing sat rotting for a couple of decades, but the 1970s saw the first efforts to restore the canal, or at least parts of it. However, this only happened after a proposal was made to fill the canal with *inoffensive sludge* from the local water treatment plant, but luckily, one rather on the ball resident realised that this roughly translated to filling it full of shit from the local sewerage works.

The locals banded together, money was raised, work slowly began, and in 1987 the first section up to Melbourne was re-opened. This work has slowly continued, and the canal-side now makes a pleasant amble for people like us and is home to a multitude of wildlife, including no less than 15 species of dragonfly and damselfly.

You can even take a boat ride along it if you wish, on the nicely restored little boat currently in front of us, which, if you remember, is called New Horizons and which is based right here. I went one day, and I was somewhat bemused when the captain allowed my little boy to take the helm, though I was not so surprised when he immediately crashed it. For some reason, my wife blamed me, but there you go. It didn't sink or anything, and there was no visible damage as I carefully surveyed it today, but it did go with a bit of a clunk.

We left the little marina behind us and crossed the bridge, and I noticed a small fingerpost sign that was just a little unusual. For some reason, it had directions to London and told us that it was 290 miles away and that you would have to go through 170 locks. That is a lot of bottles of wine, I thought to myself, and before you wonder what I am on about, I should mention that every time I have seen someone passing by on one of these things, they usually have a nice glass of red in their hands, and I don't blame them one bit.

On the same sign, another one of the fingers pointed back towards Melbourne, and it also had *nearly there* engraved upon it, which I thought was rather cute. And what do you think this bridge was called? Why, it was Swing Bridge Number Seven.

We plodded on our merry way, once again heading eastwards, and although the ground around here was certainly a bit drier, we still had to dodge the odd puddle. I was hoping that Rob would take a misstep and endure a splashy ending, but it turned out that this was to be my fate, and I felt a cold, wet trickle as water ran into my shoe.

We soon came to yet another bridge, though this one had a name. It was called Church Bridge, and it was easy to see why. It was beautiful, with flowing curves finishing in fancy round towers on either side of the canal. There was an informative sign here that tells you the bridge was built by a man called George Leather, who actually managed to build it for much less than was budgeted for after he decided to use local bricks instead of stone brought in from Leeds. This is all true, and you could forgive him for cutting corners to bring the costs down in the case of this bridge, purely and simply because the result was absolutely fantastic.

However, what the sign doesn't tell you is that George Leather was also responsible for designing and building Bilberry Reservoir, which was built in the Holme Valley, just west of Holmfirth, which had spectacularly collapsed in 1852. I had heard of this disaster when I had followed the course of the watershed up the middle of England last summer with Rob, though I had never found out who was responsible, but now I had.

Leather had been the lead architect on the design of the reservoir and the dam and had apparently cut corners there too. Specifically, he had built the dam on top of a small spring, primarily because he failed to conduct a thorough enough survey of the area. Over the years, the spring eroded away the clay base of the reservoir, leaving the dam structurally unsound. One cold February night in 1852, then, heavy rain began to fall, and water soon started to wash over the top of the dam, which had subsided due to the erosion of the spring. Eventually, the whole thing suddenly gave way, sending an estimated 86 million gallons of water hurtling down into Holmfirth.

The result was a disaster of epic proportions. Eighty people lost their lives. Seven tradesmen's houses, seven shops, seven bridges and, quite annoyingly, eight barns were destroyed in the deluge, and all fingers pointed at Leather. By 1852, however, he was an old man of 76-years, and it was also felt at the time that the disaster could possibly have been partly down to poor maintenance, although the inquest did state that the reservoir was *defective in its original construction*. Anyway, his bridge is nice.

Just after the bridge was a lock, which was closed and was overflowing with water. This meant, of course, that the land we were walking on was gradually getting higher, so hopefully, we would not encounter any more floods, at least for the time being.

We soon came across yet another bridge, Walbut Bridge, that was very similar to Church Bridge, and I mentioned to Rob that not only were the bridges better around here, but they had better names, too. There was another sign as well, with a photograph suggesting that this bridge had been comprehensively renovated in the 1980s, judging by the fashion-conscious builders that were pictured doing the work.

Plodding on, a farmer had put up a notice stating that *all dogs in field will be shot*, which seemed a bit harsh. I'm not sure of the legalities of this, but surely the dog would have to be doing something? When I checked up on this later, it is certainly the case, and any farmer who shoots a dog simply for being in a certain place would definitely find themselves on the wrong side of the law, or in legal terms, it is classed as a *civil wrong*. Whoever put that sign there should probably have their firearms licence revoked.

We moved on along the canal, passing sheep, trees and not much else. A dog walker passed us by, but she was on the other side of the canal, so we just waved to each other. This section was long and straight, as canals tend to be, but after half an hour or so, we arrived at Bielby Bend. I'm not sure if that is what this part of the canal was called, but it is certainly where the Bielby Arm is, which is a short section of canal that ventures off to the village of Bielby just a few hundred yards to the south-east. I told Rob this meant, of course, that we were going round the bend, and he replied that as he had brought two boys up, it would not be the first time.

If you cast your mind back to York, and specifically when we encountered Thomas Cooke, the astronomer, well, it was in Bielby where he opened his first school. Unfortunately, it was on the wrong side of the canal, so we could not venture there today.

We were now heading north for the first time, more or less, and the wide expanse of the Yorkshire Wolds was ahead of us in the distance. The low rolling hills seemed so far away, but they were deceptively close, and we would soon be walking up them, I promised Rob.

Before that, however, was Pocklington, just a few miles ahead of us now, but before we went there, we had decided on a small diversion. Because we had not walked all that far today, we were going to take a brief side visit to Allerthorpe, which was just a mile or two off to the west, so when we got to Coates Bridge, which was another one of George Leather's creations, though nowhere near as nice as the previous two, we followed the road into the village, which only took us half an hour or so.

I had mentioned to Rob that I wanted to make a quick diversion to Allerthorpe because as well as this being the birthplace of Thomas Cooke, who made the telescopes we heard about in York, there is a pub in the village that I wanted to visit as it had recently become a film star.

Father Christmas is Back was recently filmed in this area, a feel-good Christmas movie with some rather big-name stars, including Kelsey Grammer, Elizabeth Hurley and John Cleese. As well as putting York firmly on the map, some scenes were filmed here in Allerthorpe at the Plough Inn, so in the interest of supporting local businesses, I had suggested we pop in and say hello. It's a shame then that we walked all the way there and all the way back only to find it closed.

Nevertheless, while we were in the village, we decided to have a quick look in the rather interesting looking church dedicated to St Botolph, though as far as saints go, St Botolph was not one I had ever heard of. It turns out that St Botolph is the patron saint of boundaries. Who knew there even was one? Anyway, he is also the patron saint of travel, so it's probably good that we have popped in today. It's a shame that this was locked as well.

So it was, that over an hour after leaving Coates Bridge, we arrived back, having accomplished nothing at all really, though we did bump into an incredibly well-spoken fisherman who explained which fish you could expect to find around here. He said that tench, perch and pike were not unheard of, so when I asked him what he had caught so far, I was very surprised when he said absolutely nothing. In fact, he was packing up and going home as it was going to rain in an hour or so.

I looked at Rob, and he looked back at me, and then we both looked up at the sky. While there was certainly the odd cloud about, the sky was mainly clear, so we dismissed this foolish fisherman and carried on with our little wander.

We soon bumped into more people, this time a group of three. They were older than us, which probably made them ancient, and we chatted about this and that. They did warn us about a rather crazy swan just up ahead of us, somewhere in the vicinity of Sandhill Lock, so when we moved off, I made sure Rob was in front.

Sure enough, just a hundred yards further on, a lone swan stood guard on the bank. A young man was coming the other way, and although he moved to the side of the path furthest from the barmy bird, it still hissed at him menacingly as he passed by.

I don't think he expected it, as we heard him give a little whimper of a cry almost at the same time as he hopped away, almost skipping. It's just a bird, I said to Rob, as we said good afternoon to the wimp as he passed us by, and I must confess I was almost tempted to hiss at him, just to see what would happen.

With safety in numbers in mind, we warily approached the beautiful beast together, though, as I said, Rob was in front. The logic was that the bird would be intimidated by his huge form as well as the fact that there were two of us, either that or it would be blinded by the sunlight glinting off Rob's big shiny bald head, which would at least give us the element of surprise and the chance to slip by before he even noticed us or had time to pounce.

Unfortunately, all did not go according to plan. He stared us down, and I failed to maintain eye contact, which is probably where things first went wrong. As we were almost on top of him, the feathered fowl gave out a hiss that was certainly louder than expected. We coped with that, but then what happened next surprised us even more.

If you have never been on the noisy end of a swan, then you can count yourself lucky. They are bigger than you think, they are louder than you think, and they are scarier than you think.

And when they rise up and open their wings, well, that is truly terrifying. This one did just that as we were about as close to him as we would get, and he was huge. He hissed at the same time, which seemed even louder due to our close proximity, and I'm pretty sure I felt his spittle on my face.

Well, there was only one thing we could do. We both gave a little whimper of a cry as we hopped away, almost skipping. I think he even laughed at us.

Rob was almost running, and so was I, but the problem was that Rob was running faster than me, which meant that I would become the main course if the feathered freak behind us actually decided to attack. Luckily, he did not, but just sat there laughing, probably saying to his mate that he scared another two schmucks out of their wits today. I don't often call gracious creatures names, but that swan was a moron. I don't know how he sleeps at night.

We moved on, passing another lock, this one disused, however, and then we found another abandoned house. Ignoring the *no entry* and *trespassers will be murdered by swans* signs, we squeezed through a bit of barbed wire fencing, then climbed through a holly bush, and finally slid face-first through some nettles, all of which were presumably planted there by the owner to stop passing nosey-parkers such as ourselves. Whoever they were, they failed, and we managed to get into the garden with relatively minor scratches, burns and stings, so there.

The house was old and abandoned, and unlike the other one, which we had managed to get into without a problem, this one had all of the downstairs doors and windows bricked up.

Luckily, because Rob was so tall, he could more or less see through the upstairs windows anyway, but unfortunately, there was still nothing to see. After round two of suicide-by-plant, we were back on the path and once more heading for Pocklington.

We must have been getting near the main road as we could hear traffic every now and then through the trees, and on top of this, the path became slightly more well-kept.

Someone had cut the hedges and the grass, and after we went through a gate, we were at Pocklington Canal Head, a small picnic area complete with benches, information signs and even a toilet. We were glad to see all of these, particularly the latter, and after making use of them all, we ambled slowly towards the road.

A couple of people passed us, who both said hello, and we stopped to look at a small plaque. It told the story of a Lancaster bomber that crashed nearby in 1943, that had taken off from Lincolnshire for a bombing raid on Berlin. When it returned, it was diverted up here due to fog, and after being unable to land at Melbourne, where we had just come from, it attempted to land at Pocklington airfield, literally just across the road from here. Sadly, it never made it and ran out of fuel, crashing into some houses just behind the pub in front of us.

The plaque doesn't tell the full story, though. That same night, Catherine Ross and her younger sister Evelyn had been to a dance in Pocklington. They had returned home to their house in Ramsdale Terrace, just across the road, which was just behind the Wellington Oak pub. While the pub is still there, the row of houses has long since gone. Anyway, when Catherine and Evelyn returned home and were getting ready for bed, they felt an almighty shake. Catherine ran across the bedroom and opened the blackout curtains, and what she saw horrified her. A ball of flames had engulfed the house of their neighbour, Gertrude Bird, and the scene was unrecognisable. Evelyn ran to alert her father, who immediately got dressed and ran across to help, as did the landlord of the pub, Mr Blades.

All in all, seven people died that night, including five airmen, Mrs Bird, and her lodger, Percy Hopkinson. Sadly, all of the flight crew who died were only in their twenties. As for the house, most of the front was gone but was later rebuilt, and it is the white one on the corner with two chimneys and is called Ings House. When the accident occurred, the Lancaster deposited one of its engines in the bedroom of a nearby farmhouse, and if you look closely at this house, which is now called the Mill House, there are several wall plates that were added when the building was repaired. Don't do what we did, though, and just wander into the garden for a nosey, because they have a rather large dog with big pointy teeth. Still, that's better than a deranged swan, isn't it?

We crossed the main road, and the path took us through a small farmyard before immediately belching us out into a grassy meadow. The sun was in and out of the clouds, but it was still behind us on this final leg into Pocklington. We only had a couple of miles to go and reckoned we would be there within the hour, until that is, we ran into the man in the meadow.

The encounter started fairly normally, as most encounters tend to do, I guess. He was walking his dog, which bizarrely was another labrador cross that reminded me of my beautiful Belle. He was throwing a ball for the dog to fetch back, a green one, and he seemed like a fairly normal bloke, and I heard him say that the dog was called Amber.

However, this normality was shattered within a couple of minutes of the conversation starting. I blame Rob, as he actually initiated the conversation due to being thirty feet ahead of me, mentioning to the guy that his dog was similar to mine.

Actually, it may have been my fault, as when I caught them up, I simply said hello and asked him if he was okay. He looked at me and said that no, he wasn't, as he had actual knowledge of what was really going on.

This puzzled me, and when I looked at Rob, he looked just as mystified as me.

The man then went on, and oh boy, did he go on. He told us about the illuminati, about certain politicians and billionaires who will shortly be executed for their actions, he told us about magical plants on Japanese islands that can make you live forever, and how he had just bought some, and lots more crap that I can't even remember.

Rob had already started to edge slowly backwards, clearly alarmed by the lunatic detector that was apparently going off in his head. However, on the other hand, I felt like a rabbit caught in the headlines. A small part of me wanted to run with this conversation, just to see where it went, but then the sensible side of me wanted to actually run. I should have run away as well because there was simply no getting away after that. All I could think was that everyone has the right to be stupid, but judging by this example, some abuse that privilege.

I'm not sure how much of my life I spent there, but it certainly felt like a lot more than it actually was, and I was only able to get away when his dog ran off looking for the ball, which, if you remember, was green, and was now, luckily for me, lost somewhere within a field full of green plants.

Rob, who had somehow tiptoed around a hundred yards further along the path, was laughing his head off, but when I caught up with him, I tore a strip off him and questioned our brotherly bond of never leaving a man behind. He just laughed even more.

As we walked off, a young lady appeared with her even younger daughter, and they too had a labrador cross, and they were heading towards the crazy old man. There must be a labrador farm around here, suggested Rob.

Not wanting to let her walk into a trap, I warned her about the old crazy guy and how I had just lost a considerable amount of my life that I would never be able to get back, ever, before kneeling down to pet her dog. It was very friendly, as are most labradors, and I asked her what it was called.

In a sterner than expected voice, she replied that this dog was called Ruby, and in fact, Ruby was Amber's sister. Furthermore, she added, and in an even angrier voice, the crazy old man was her father. More specifically, and in an even angrier voice, she added that the crazy old man was her daughter's grandfather, and she now looked visibly upset because some smelly hiker had basically called her grandad a lunatic. I think

Rob actually wet himself laughing, and while I wished for a hole to open up in the earth and swallow me up, this didn't happen, so after apologising profusely around a thousand times, I followed Rob, hanging my head in shame in the process.

A small stream ran on our left, and we were heading upriver towards lots of new houses. A planning notice was stuck to a tree, and when I went over to check it out, it announced that this meadow would soon be yet another housing estate, which was sad, as it was so nice. I imagined that the small stream would not be quite so picturesque in a couple of years, but that is just the way the cookie crumbles, I guess.

We crossed a small road and suddenly found ourselves in suburbia. The contrast was intense, as we now found ourselves standing among faceless and identical houses. Don't get me wrong, they were all pretty nice; it's just that they were, well, all the same. You would think that architects would spice things up a bit nowadays; I know I would. Something a bit unexpected every now and then, just to make sure the planning inspector is paying attention. Maybe one that looked like a pyramid, or perhaps an upside-down house, or even one that looked like a spaceship. Basically, anything other than these characterless boxes that we all seem to live in nowadays.

We wandered through a snicket and caught up with a very frail and elderly couple walking a tiny dog. It was almost a teddy bear, and when I asked the lady what kind of dog it was, I didn't quite catch what she said, but it sounded like *oopsie-doopsie*, which was good enough for me. The gentleman was clearly struggling to walk, and he said that he had recently had his hips and knees replaced, and he said he felt like a new man. Anything goes in the 21st century, I said, winking at his wife.

The dog, he added, could walk for miles, and it was very friendly, judging by what it was trying to do to Rob's leg. Revenge is a very sweet thing indeed, I thought to myself, as my mind wandered to the mad man of the meadow and how Rob had abandoned me to my fate. I made sure we spoke for several minutes more, and once the dog had finished what he had been doing and finally went to lean against a lamp-post and lit a cigarette, I knew it was time to move on.

A shortcut led us into the cemetery, and far from being dead, it was a hive of activity. Several men were chopping trees down while others put the branches through a wood-chipper, and further along, someone was digging a hole, though there was no need to explain that, of course.

One memorial, in particular, caught my eye,

and it was in the form of a horse. It had been placed next to a bench and had clearly become someone's special place, but I didn't read the inscription as I just knew it would be very sad indeed. Instead, we carried on and went to look at the chapel at the far end of the cemetery.

It actually turned out to be two chapels, so this must have been a very busy place at one time or another. I opened the gate to go and get a closer look but then more or less immediately realised that the chapels were no longer chapels but had been converted into houses.

The squeaky gate must have alerted the owner as the curtains twitched, and inside I could see an angry-looking face staring back at me. I gave my best wave of apology and retreated back out of the garden, half expecting the door to open, but it never did.

We were more or less in the centre of Pocklington now, and after leaving the cemetery behind, we immediately found ourselves on a busy shopping park, with heavy traffic and lots of people coming and going. This was in stark contrast to the rest of our walk, which had been along leafy lanes and empty paths, not to mention the tranquillity of the walk along the canal. I say tranquillity, but I think it was fair to say that we were both still traumatised by that bloody swan, in all honesty.

Anyway, we wanted to look at a couple of things in Pocklington. The first was the school, as this is where William Wilberforce was educated, and the second was the church.

We found the school easily enough. Although it would have changed significantly since Wilberforce's days, when he presumably spent his time doodling with his quill and vandalising his wooden desk, you can still get a sense of what the place would have been like back then. We had a quick look at the site, but didn't stay too long, primarily because we didn't want to get arrested, which I imagine is something that tends to happen to grown men that hang around schools.

They have a couple of interesting statues, though. The first one is of a slave, seated and in manacles, though curiously, the manacles are open, presumably representing freedom. There is a second statue, this one of Wilberforce, though unlike other statues of him, it depicts him in his childhood, which makes sense considering this was his school. We found the statue of Wilberforce without a problem, but despite having a good look, we couldn't find the other one, which was a shame, but as I said, we didn't want to get arrested.

William Wilberforce is obviously the most famous past pupil that the school likes to go on about when trying to attract new talent, and they even refer to him as The Greatest

Yorkshireman. I'm not sure I quite agree on that one, though, as that would make him better than Michael Palin, who was actually awarded that title just a few years back and is very well-deserved, in my opinion at least. Anyway, there are, in fact, many more who went on to live notable lives. Adrian Edmondson, an actor famous for appearing in the sitcom *The Young Ones*, is one of the more notable, along with top-flight tennis player Kyle Edmund.

Sebastian Horsley is another one, and while you may not have heard of him, he's a very interesting guy. He is a former prostitute turned artist and writer and has led quite a life. He was once actually deported from America for moral turpitude, which basically meant they knew he had taken drugs at some point in his life, which is a bit rich coming from America.

Way back in 2000, he travelled to the Philippines, who did let him in, and he went so he could experience a crucifixion. Confused? Well, I mean exactly what I say. He had himself nailed to a cross, just for the fun of it, in order to prepare for a series of paintings on the topic.

He mostly lived in London during his adult life, quite possibly in the dodgy part, as he had a sign on his door saying *this is not a brothel,* and he lived in high circles indeed. He died in 2010, and the likes of Stephen Fry and Marc Bolan paid tribute to him at his funeral, where his coffin was carried out of the church to the tune of T-Rex's *20th Century Boy*, and it is fair to say that he truly was one.

Ralph Ineson is another one, and he is an actor who has been in everything from Game of Thrones to Harry Potter and much else in between, including Guardians of the Galaxy, Kingsman: The Secret Service, Coronation Street, Peaky Blinders and lots more besides. Although he might not be that well-known by name, you would know him if you saw him.

And finally, Charles McMoran is another one, who later became Lord Moran and was the personal physician of none other than Winston Churchill. It is perhaps no surprise, then, to find out that Pocklington School is a private school and demands fees of several thousand pounds each term in return for educating your little darlings, but judging by the list of past pupils, perhaps it's worth it?

Our last port of call was the church, or more specifically, the churchyard. You may have guessed by now that I like to seek out the stories that are, how shall we put it, a little weird, and as you may also have guessed, this is exactly the direction we were going now, which brings us rather nicely to the strange tales of William Richardson and Thomas Pelling.

Let us first of all deal with the tale of William

Richardson, who was born in the town in 1797. What the history books will tell you about Richardson is that he was a famous astronomer, who went to work at the Greenwich Observatory, and he was even awarded a Gold Medal from the Royal Astronomical Society. While this is all true, what they won't tell you, is that Richardson also slept with his own daughter, managed to get her pregnant, and then found himself arrested and on trial for the murder of his own son. Come to think of it, the child might technically have been his grandson, or was possibly even both? While this might sound a bit bizarre, incest wasn't even a crime back then, and he probably would have gotten away with it had he not buried the child in his own garden, where it was later discovered by a labourer who was digging out a cesspool.

Anyway, finding himself sacked from his job due to this self-inflicted scandal, he spent the rest of his life in relative obscurity. This was not a problem, though, as he had made rather a lot of money and owned several properties in the town, one of which was the Star Inn, which once stood in the marketplace, and which itself gained notoriety following a rather funny but clearly tragic accident in 1733, which brings us on to Thomas Pelling.

Thomas Pelling, you see, was a flying man, which meant he was really just a showman who travelled the region performing feats of bravery in exchange for money. While in Pocklington, Pelling tied a rope from the top of the church tower to the Star Inn. The plan was to dress like a bat, seriously, and glide down the rope, thereby amazing everybody below and hopefully generating lots of lovely cash donations in the process.

The trick didn't quite go to plan, however, and Pelling instead fell straight to his death, ironically landing right in the middle of the churchyard. They buried him where he fell, and they didn't even have to dig that much of a hole, really, as he hit the soft ground so hard, he more or less made his own grave. In typical Yorkshire fashion, they just kicked a bit of dirt over him and went back into the pub. In some of the best old English I had read in a while, the parish register says, and I quote, *Thomas Pelling . . . was killed by jumping against ye Battlement of ye Choir when coming down ye Rope from ye Steeple.*

Ye not kidding, as they say in Yorkshire. I wondered what the last thing was that went through Pelling's mind as he registered what was going to happen, and then I realised that it was the ground. There is an ornamental plaque detailing these events on the outside wall of the church near the east window, which recounts this story exactly as I have said it, so at least you know I am not lying, although the bit about him hitting the ground and making his own hole might be just a little white lie. Anyway, he really is buried exactly where he fell. The pub is gone now, which is a shame, put out of business when it burned down in 1845, but the building survived and later became shops. As for the flying man, Pocklington has recently revived the Flying Man Festival, which sees hot air balloons and an air show entertain people from far and wide, but hopefully does not have someone launching themselves directly at the floor from the top of the church.

Pelling wasn't alone in his exploits. It would appear that in December of the same year, another flying man was busy entertaining the crowds with a similar trick, this time up in Newcastle. His journey started at the top of the castle and ended in Baileygate, and originally all went well. However, for some unfathomable reason, the gentleman in question then decided to repeat the trick with, wait for it, his donkey. You can probably imagine from the mere fact that I included it here that all did not go well, and you would be right. Several people were injured, and one girl was killed when the donkey hit the crowd, though there is no record of how the beast fared in all of this. You could not make this stuff up.

However, the most famous of these flying men was Robert Cadman, who became known as the *Icarus of the rope*. Just like his namesake, things didn't end well for Cadman. He gained a reputation for flying down some of the steepest steeples in the country, but his luck started to run out in 1735 when he actually managed to bring down a tower in Wiltshire and subsequently crashed into a tree. Undaunted, he was soon off again, this time from the top of St Mary's in Shrewsbury. Unfortunately, the rope was too tight, and when it snapped, he plummeted into the crowd, injuring several others and killing himself.

And lastly, on Pocklington, while we have already heard that Adrian Edmondson went to school here, we should note that he is on record as calling it crap, though I think he meant the school, not the town. And if you've ever had a Terry's Chocolate Orange, then the Terry in question, Joseph Terry, was born right here in Pocklington, too, so there.

As we found ourselves finally at the end of our walk for the day, we felt the first spots of rain, proving the fisherman right, and which, let's face it, was great timing, particularly as we were still covered in manure, or at least our feet were. We never did see a black labrador, and we wondered if someone is still wandering around Melbourne to this very day with his empty lead in his hand. And as for the lady we met while walking into Pocklington, I am so sorry for insulting your

father, but you really do need to keep him off the
internet.

The Yorkshire Giant

Pocklington to Market Weighton

The weather gods had abandoned us, apart perhaps, from Neptune and Poseidon. As we stood at a bus stop in Market Weighton, a gentle drizzle fell all around us, showering everything with the finest aquatic coating known to man.

Today's plan was to get the bus back to Pocklington, where we had finished last time, and walk back to the car which we had left parked rather precariously at the entrance to the small town-centre car park. I say precariously, as the space we had occupied was adjacent to the entrance, and even before we had left it behind, two cars had swung by, missing it by mere inches. I didn't particularly want to leave it there, but that space had been the only one available, and it was easy to see why judging by the remnants of what might once have been a wing mirror lying strewn across the tarmac.

This was not the best start to the day then, and on top of that, the bus never came. We stood beneath a shelter for a while, trying to keep out of the rain, and I finally wandered across the road to ask someone who looked like a local whether we were in the right place. We certainly were, they said, but the buses were always late, apparently.

Obviously, with that, the bus appeared, and I found myself on the wrong side of a now busy road. It was an interesting game I played as I put my life in my hands trying to get back across, and it reminded me of an old computer game I used to enjoy. I half-expected a crocodile to appear in between the cars, but sadly, there were none.

The bus took an interesting route, generally following the main road, but every now and then, it would dart off to one village or another that we never even knew existed. I had mentioned to Rob that I was surprised how many people were aboard, and he replied that yes, it was rather full, and also that he had noticed we were probably the youngest people on board, which is really quite saying something, as we're no spring chickens ourselves.

The windows were totally steamed up, so

there was not much to see, although this did give any budding artists the chance to create a temporary masterpiece. Indeed, someone had done exactly this and had drawn what looked like a pair of boobs on the window next to me. Rob obviously thought that I had done it, but as he never actually saw me, I denied all knowledge and said his evidence was flimsy at best and purely circumstantial.

The bus dumped us in Pocklington after just twenty minutes or so, which was actually much quicker than expected. The rain was coming down here, too, so we both took advantage of the shelter at the bus stop and changed into our wet gear. I had brought my silly hat, the wide-brimmed one, and intended to do my best Indiana Jones impression today, while Rob had a woolly hat on, which would mean his head would eventually get wet, I told him, with more than a hint of glee, I must say.

A young lady watched us change and asked us if we were going far. She looked like a walker herself and was dressed for the part today, and she even had her hiking poles. When we told her we were going back to Market Weighton, she told us she had been near Londesborough a couple of days previously and said that although the paths beyond the village were sort of passable, it would help if we enjoyed swimming or had remembered to bring a canoe. I'm not sure if she was joking, but she wasn't smiling.

We bade her farewell and made our way into town, which was a bustling hive of activity and much busier than expected. We didn't really stop to look in any shops, though when we found a local bakery, we felt totally obliged to support the local economy as we tend to do wherever we go, and Rob went in and grabbed us both one of the largest Cornish pasties I had seen in quite a while.

We ate on the go, making our way through the town and leaving a trail of crumbs, and soon found ourselves on a narrow back-road which seemed to be taking us out of the place. There was little of note along this little road until we came across a small bar with the rather unusual and highly entertaining name of *The Stumble Inn*. It's a shame that it was so early in the morning, I mentioned to Rob, as we could have supported the local economy some more, and he wholeheartedly agreed.

Turning away from the main road and through a small housing estate where the townhouses seemed to be crammed impossibly close together, we joined a small footpath and got the impression that we would soon be out in the open countryside, but after just a few dozen yards, we were on yet another estate, and navigating our way through a warren of small paths and roads that nearly saw us get lost.

Finally, however, we seemed to leave Pocklington behind for good, as we were greeted with a muddy path that did not look in any way urban. However, the path in question wanted to take us up a big hill, which did not really seem fair at such an early hour, though really, we had no choice. A sign pointed to Kilnwick Percy and told us it was just over a mile away, so we simply put our heads down and moved on.

We slipped and slid as we made our way up, and Rob did better than me as he had remembered to bring his hiking poles. Dodging deep-looking puddles that promised an early morning surprise if either of us took a tumble, we found ourselves skirting one edge of the path and then jumping to the other side to repeat our acrobatics.

Several men wearing hi-vis vests were busy building a rather large house on the hill below us, one of those that seem to feature on television programs and cost several million pounds. It wasn't a day to be doing this, though, and they all looked miserable in the constant rain.

Almost immediately after leaving the concrete paths of Pocklington, I felt my feet getting wet and realised I had, quite stupidly, put my old walking shoes on today. This was a rookie error of epic proportions, as I had more or less destroyed this pair on the rocky slopes of Loch Lomond last year, and they now had several holes in them. The holes were only small, but water doesn't need much, I thought to myself, as I felt the moisture slowly making its way around my entire foot.

We slipped and slid along, almost as if we were skiing, and we were very happy when the gradient levelled out and the path became more or less flat. There were probably some good views to our right, I mentioned to Rob, not that we could see anything today, of course. Low cloud brought the visibility down to just a few hundred feet, and although we could see a little bit of the town below us and behind us, that was about all we could see today.

The puddles became worse, and although I tried to dodge them as much as I could, it was impossible to avoid them all. Rob was doing better than me at this early point, as not only did he have his poles, but he also had his new boots on, which he reminded me were definitely waterproof.

A sign up ahead promised a distraction, and it was one of those historical information boards you find dotted here and there, and this one was a corker. It was all about the Pilgrimage of Grace, which, if you did not know, was a rebellion that started right here, in Yorkshire.

It happened during the reign of King Henry VIII, in 1536 to be precise, after the despotic king had increased taxes, closed the monasteries, and cancelled public holidays. He had also buried one wife, Catherine of Aragon, beheaded another, Anne Boleyn, and then more or less immediately married a third, Jayne Seymour, so not surprisingly, everyone thought he had gone absolutely and completely stark raving mad.

Breaking away from the Catholic Church was also seen as something of a problem, and the closure of the monasteries caused more difficulties than many of us realise and for all sorts of reasons. Monasteries, at the time, you see, acted as hotels, schools and hospitals, and also served as a kind of social services, caring for the poorest in society, and it was this act that was the last straw and which forced the rebellion that became the Pilgrimage of Grace.

The rebellion actually began in Beverley, which is, of course, one of our later stops on the Wilberforce Way. When the number of angry citizens increased to sufficient numbers to give rebels the courage to move on, they went to Market Weighton Hill in October 1536, where their numbers swelled even more and where they first coined the name Pilgrimage of Grace. A Yorkshireman and lawyer called Robert Aske became their leader, and while not a lot is known about him, we do know that he was blind in one eye. Aske was also assisted by Sir Robert Constable, another local landowner who had become disillusioned with the king.

The majority of the rebels then made a move on York, which they took without having to fire a shot, while a smaller detachment went to capture Hull, although they had to fight to take the town, because if you remember, the people of Hull are, well, awkward.

Anyway, there were now around 50,000 rebels, and their next move was on the royal army near Doncaster. Unfortunately, the king only had around 8,000 troops of his own, led by Thomas Howard, the Duke of Norfolk, who knew the game was up and that he could not win. Instead, he offered a truce that included a Royal Pardon for those involved in what was technically treason, and he also offered to halt the king's most unpopular policies and hold a Parliament at York in order to address the Pilgrim grievances.

Aske and Constable were both given guarantees of safety, but only Aske travelled down to London for direct talks with the king, as Constable smartly declined the invitation. For a while, all looked well, but it is important to point out that at no time was the Duke of Norfolk authorised to negotiate in the manner that he did, and it is likely that he did so simply because his forces were outnumbered and he didn't want to get chopped into tiny little pieces.

Regardless, the rebels agreed to the truce based on the conditions set out by the duke, and while they were certainly men of honour, unfortunately, the king was not. When a couple of minor insurrections broke out later, the king used this as an excuse to arrest all of those originally involved in the Pilgrimage of Grace, executed them, and then swept the whole thing under the carpet, where it remained almost forgotten for centuries.

Robert Aske had actually been on his way back up north when the king had him arrested, after which he was taken to the Tower of London. As soon as he was convicted of treason at Westminster, he was hanged on a special scaffold built especially for him at the base of Clifford's Tower in York. The fact that this was done at York was intended to send a signal to anyone else who had any foolish ideas about freedom or justice.

Although Constable had declined the king's invitation to travel to London, he too was eventually captured. The Duke of Norfolk travelled back up north and promptly arrested him and had him hanged at the Beverley Gate in Hull on Friday 6th July. The date was no coincidence, as Friday was market day in Hull, thus ensuring that as many people as possible saw what could happen to even the highest members of society, again ensuring that nobody else got any silly ideas. Norfolk was recorded as saying that Constable was so trimmed in chains his body would probably hang there for a hundred years.

In total, 216 people were executed in connection with the uprising, including several lords and knights, 7 abbots, 38 monks, 16 priests, and a partridge in a pear tree, probably. This high death toll is perhaps partly down to the fact that some people involved in the rebellion tried to implicate the Duke of Norfolk, who had quite possibly been somewhat sympathetic to the cause at some point, so he was forced to kill more or less everyone else if he wished to save his own skin.

What goes around comes around, though, and in December 1546, Thomas Howard, the Duke of Norfolk, was himself arrested along with his son Henry, and they were both sent to the same tower that he had previously sent so many others to. At his trial, if that's what you can call it, his own wife and daughter gave evidence against him, as well as his mistress, a woman called Bess Holland.

The king signed death warrants for both him and his son and added a cruel caveat that meant the duke would have to watch his son die first. Henry was executed on the 19th of January 1547, with the duke's execution set for the 28th of January. However, anyone who knows their history may well know that Henry VIII himself died on the 28th of January 1547, and it is exactly this that saved the Duke of Norfolk's life, as it was considered bad form to inaugurate a new reign with bloodshed.

However, the ascent to the throne of Edward VI did not spell the end of the duke's problems. The new king was only nine years old when he took the crown, and the Duke of Norfolk stayed right where he was, in prison. He was only released when Queen Mary took office in 1553, but his imprisonment had taken a heavy toll on him, and he died shortly after in 1554.

As we read the sign that told us much of this story, rain dripped on us from the trees above, so we soon moved off, once more dodging puddle after puddle. Kilnwick Percy golf course stood to our left, and not surprisingly, it was deserted today. We hopped through the hedge a little later on and followed the public footpath across the greens, thankful for the bad weather, which meant we would not have to risk dying today due to being hit on the head with a golf ball. We might drown instead, I pointed out to Rob, as much of the spongy surface of the golf course was under rather a lot of water.

A sign told us we should look left and right at all times, which Rob pointed out was technically impossible when you think about it. It also told us that if we heard someone shout the word *fore*, we should prepare to die, or at least prepare to suffer mild brain damage, which made me wonder why people put footpaths across golf courses? I've never been hit by a golf ball when crossing one, but I've come uncomfortably close, and while there might not be all that much going on in this little head of mine, I don't really want it cracked open like an egg, thank you very much.

As we moved on, my shoes continued to soak up impressive amounts of water, but I had given up caring, as I imagined they could not get much wetter. When I mentioned this to Rob, he helpfully let me know that his feet were still nice and dry, largely down to the fact that he was not stupid and had not worn old shoes with holes in that day. Sometimes his comments are not helpful at all, I told him, to which he replied that he knew this and that I was welcome.

We hit the road at the other side of the golf course and decided to take in a quick detour. Although our path should technically take us north and around Kilnwick Hall, we had instead decided to cut through the grounds of the hall. The distance would be much the same but would take a much more interesting route, and I mentioned to Rob that I couldn't understand why the path didn't go that way anyway.

After a quick hop across the road, then, we were soon on the driveway of the beautiful old house that was Kilnwick Percy Hall, which is now a meditation centre, apparently. Despite the weather, there were still a few people coming and going from the hall, and on more than one occasion, we had to jump on the grass verge to allow passing traffic to go by.

An impressive mound stood to our north, presumably some kind of burial mound, and it was now surrounded by several pine trees, but I imagined that whichever ancient human was within it must have been pretty important to someone, as it was huge.

As we got nearer to the hall, someone had seemingly lost a glove. By the time that we left the scene, the glove was on the top of a nearby fingerpost and was fitted so as to make an interesting and rather well-known gesture usually involving the middle finger. I'm not saying who did it, but it was probably the same person that childishly drew boobs on the inside of a bus window earlier that day. Rob shook his head in shame, but I think he was just jealous that he never thought of it first.

A sign announced the name of the place, as it was no longer Kilnwick Percy Hall, apparently, but was now known by the much easier to pronounce name of Madhyamaka Kadampa Meditation Centre. I'm not sure why they call it Madhyamaka, as it did not make me mad at all, and indeed I have enjoyed several peaceful walks here over the years.

A couple of my previous visits particularly stand out. The first was when my wife and I brought our young son here, who must have been around five at the time. As five-year-olds tend to be, he was basically a lunatic, and he just had endless energy. We tried to tire him out by walking him all around the grounds, but that did not work, and my wife refused to let me take him on the golf course so the golferists could use him as target practice, which would at least buy us a couple of hours of peace and quiet until he regained consciousness.

Instead, we took him to the café, which is where we bumped into his primary school teacher, who had just happened to come to the meditation centre for a bit of peace and quiet herself, as well as to recover from teaching a class of five-year-old psychopaths the previous week. Well, suffice to say, that was the end of her peace and quiet when he screamed *hello* across the courtyard of the café and then ran over to give her a big hug. I think she saw the funny side.

The second incident involved my older child and occurred on a hot summer day. I'm not going to name which one of my kids it was, but the one in question was busy taking a couple of selfies and had decided to lay across my car. The sun was out, and he did actually look rather cool in his sunglasses, and all was well until he rolled off the car, leaving behind a rather large teenager shaped dent in the bodywork. Needless to say, I wasn't very happy, and when I got home, I found a hammer in the shed with the bright idea of knocking the dent back out again. I thought it would be pretty straightforward, and it would just pop back into shape with a little encouragement from my whacking stick, but by the time I had finished, my car looked like it had gone ten rounds with Mike Tyson.

Thankfully, there was none of that today, though. In fact, there were no children around at all, which was a blessing. A couple of dog walkers were down by the lake, and one gentleman had very bravely allowed his black labrador to go for a swim. Rather him than me, I thought, as I recalled my own dog doing the same thing on the James Herriot Way just a couple of months before. Let's just say the smell had been *interesting*.

Anyway, the hall was very beautiful, even in the rain, and it also had a bit of history. Of particular interest was what looked like a Second World War bunker hidden just behind the fancy golden sign that welcomed you to the hall. I had seen bunkers like this before, or more accurately, I had seen pictures of bunkers like this, and if it was what I thought it was, it would be an amazing find.

During the war, and with Nazi Germany practically kicking down the door, everyone thought that an invasion was imminent. In order to ensure that the country could carry on the fight even after the Germans had arrived, special resistance units were set up by the government. Although these were given the rather boring name of Auxiliary Units, they were basically the building blocks of a massive resistance movement that would hit enemy targets following any occupation.

The units were initially based at Benningholme Hall and then Rise Hall and were led by Captain Peter Hollis, son of the vicar of Hornsea. Because Rise was rather close to the sea, the headquarters were soon moved to Middleton Hall near Driffield. Now led by Captain Terry Leigh-Lye, as Hollis had gone off to East Africa to shoot actual enemy troops, the unit used the hall's stables as their headquarters, although it is said that they held most of their meetings at the nearby local pub, the Crown and Anchor. However, this might be misinformation, as the only pub I could find in the village when I checked was the Rose and Crown.

Perhaps somewhat surprisingly, they would not just have targeted enemy combatants, but they were also given secret orders to assassinate weak links who might inadvertently give away vital intelligence if interrogated or even betray the existence and locations of the auxiliary units themselves. For instance, there were many local policemen, and I am afraid it was just men in those days, who might have been on the kill list simply because it was them who would have carried out background checks on the men assigned to the auxiliary units and would thus know the names and addresses of those involved, putting everyone at risk.

They may also have had to kill their own superiors, such as Hollis and Leigh-Lye, once hostilities commenced because these men would have known of the existence, locations and the names of the members of many of the auxiliary units and were, therefore, a severe security risk should they be captured. And even innocent passers-by would have been killed had they been unfortunate enough to stumble across one of these hidden bunkers.

I would not have been much good at all of this. It's not that I can't keep a secret because I can. It's just that all of the people I share them with simply can't. And anyway, women might actually be better at this than us men. I had recently read that scientists have discovered how women keep their secrets. They do so within groups of 40.

Anyway, I strongly suspected that this bunker was one of those that would have been used by these units. When I later approached Kilnwick Percy Hall asking about the bunker, they were able to confirm that the building had indeed been requisitioned during the war but did not have many details on what actually went on here or what the bunker was for. They also told me that the bunker was strictly off-limits and I was not to go near it again, which made me feel like a naughty schoolboy caught with his hand in the cookie jar.

After a fair bit of digging, though, if you pardon the pun, I was able to confirm that the whole site was used to train members of the special forces, despite the army saying that it was used as a sorting office for forces mail, but then they would say that, wouldn't they? Obviously, due to the nature of the work, not many historical records exist about this sort of thing, and all of those involved have now passed away, so we may never know the truth for sure. Sadly, also due to the secretive nature of the work, the men who had formed these units were never recognised and thus did not receive the Defence Medal that was given to all of the other branches of the Home Services, an injustice that, although largely forgiven, was certainly never forgotten by many of them.

Lastly, one final note is worthy regarding Captain Peter Hollis. The war must have had quite an impact on him, and after the war, he became a man of the cloth, with a rather nice church and a large congregation in Birmingham. He was also a founding member of

Amnesty International and strongly supported the Campaign for Nuclear Disarmament as well as the anti-apartheid movement. He even found himself getting told off by his own church after helping to organise a bus trip in support of peace protestors at Greenham Common, which housed nuclear-tipped cruise missiles for many years during the 1980s.

And very lastly on this, the soldiers in charge of the hall clearly had a good time while they were billeted here, whatever they were doing. While it may never be known what exactly they actually did get up to, they clearly had some fun, judging by the fact that they nearly burned the place down, although, in the end, the damage was thankfully limited to one half of the original grand staircase.

The history of Kilnwick Percy goes back a lot further than that, though. Way back in 1066, when William of Normandy, who we already came across just after leaving York, of course, first invaded our lovely little island, he took the land around what is now the hall from the previous owner, Morcar, Earl of Northumberland, who if you remember, we also last heard about at the Battle of Fulford. William subsequently gifted the land and the hall that stood on it to a man called Robert de Bruis, who was the three times great grandfather to the much more famous Robert the Bruce of

Scotland, although he would never know this himself, of course. I mean, how can anyone know their great-great-great grandkids, and more importantly, why would anyone want to?

And if we are going back any further, then we might want to remember the mound that we saw on the way in, which actually turns out to be a hill barrow, which was once excavated by a local archaeologist called John Robert Mortimer. Mortimer excavated almost every interesting lump and bump that he could find in and around East Yorkshire, and he built up an impressive collection of artifacts. Although he had always been a prolific collector, one of the reasons he became so successful was that he utilised a new invention that no one else had thought to do.

High scale Ordnance Survey maps had recently become available, and Mortimer was able to scour the countryside with these maps in minutes in order to find potential archaeological sites, rather than spend weeks on the road doing exactly the same thing and just getting tired legs and muddy feet. On top of this, because Mortimer had grown up on a farm, he learned to recognise the clues offered by the land, such as changes in the colours of vegetation and crops signalling the presence of prehistoric features and ditches and the like.

With his many finds, he initially opened up a museum in his home town of Driffield, but this closed when he went bankrupt in 1887, which was partly caused by the repeal of the corn laws and the subsequent low price of crops. His collection was sold, but luckily it found its way to a museum in Hull, where it can still be seen to this day, or at least some of it can. It holds around 66,000 items, so there is probably nowhere big enough to actually show all of it.

We should be grateful that it was Mortimer who excavated this and many other mounds around here, rather than his regular partner, the Canon William Greenwell, an unusual combination of a man who was part archaeologist, part priest, and part moron. Greenwell more or less operated a scorched earth policy when digging much of the land around here and was much criticised by others in the field, if you pardon the pun, for his poor excavation techniques.

Mortimer, on the other hand, was much lauded for his use of the scientific method and has even been described as one of the first rescue archaeologists, due to his intense desire to gain and preserve the knowledge of the ancient inhabitants of our lands. He was also said to be one of the seminal figures responsible for the birth of British archaeology, too, so there you go, something else to thank Yorkshire for.

He certainly seems to have done a good job here, anyway. The mound looked intact, and to the untrained eye at least, it did not look like it had ever been disturbed, to be honest.

We wandered around the side of the house, just for a look, really, and I was momentarily surprised when through one of the windows, I saw someone that looked like a monk vacuuming, though it was actually a monk hoovering up. I reckon I was simply surprised because this is not something I had ever seen before, and in fact, this is not something you see every day, but bearing in mind that this place is now a Buddhist retreat and that the carpets would not clean themselves, I guess somebody had to do it.

We wandered down to the small church, which was fenced off and was only for the use of the monks, so instead, we followed a sign which pointed back to the hall. On the way, we bumped into the dog walker we had seen earlier, along with his very wet dog, which was very playful and generous and insisted on sharing his pond water with us both. To be honest, we were incredibly wet and muddy ourselves, which probably meant that if anyone was going to make someone else dirtier, it was actually us and not the dog.

The gentleman called the dog Ruby, meaning this was the second dog we had met with this name on our walk, though this guy was somewhat saner than the previous one and he did at least live on the same planet as us. We had a nice chat about the weather and other trivial stuff, but he also gave us a good tip, which was to make sure we visited the walled garden before we left.

The walled garden was exactly as advertised, a garden with a wall. I guess it was very nice, but as it was the middle of winter and it was chucking it down with rain still, we decided not to stop for a picnic on this occasion, but I imagined it would be great in summer.

We finally left the hall and gardens behind and joined a small road which took us east and up a rather sharp hill. Turning right at a crossroads, we immediately found ourselves going downhill, which seemed to make the uphill part that we had just done rather pointless. I mean, what is the point of going up and down just for the sake of it, I said to Rob, to which he replied that there wasn't much point unless, of course, you're having sex.

Anyway, this looked like it would continue for some time, as a cartoon-like road twisted ahead of us, and I almost expected a road-runner to appear, which would at least have been a bit more exciting than today's wet walk.

Even the sheep in the fields were trying to hide away from the weather, some having taken shelter in what looked like a pig pen just a few yards from the road.

Rounding a bend and coming to a farm, someone had built a small summer house by the side of the road, and we were surprised to see a young man sitting inside it. As we approached, he opened the door and waved to us, and asked if we were going far. He seemed surprised when we said we were heading for Market Weighton, and he helpfully told us that it was a bit wet today. I thanked him and told him I hadn't realised, but I don't think he noticed my sarcasm, to be honest.

He worked on the farm, he told us, and said he was having a break until the rain stopped, or at least lightened off a bit, and he laughed when I told him he would probably be back at work sometime in May then, or perhaps June, if he was really lucky.

He also confirmed what I think we both already knew. We were the first walkers he had seen today, he went on, though what he actually meant was we were really very stupid for being out in this weather and, in fact, we were probably several times more stupid than your average walker, and much wetter as well.

To be honest, it was only my feet which were wet, as my waterproofs were actually doing a great job of keeping the rest of me dry. Rob was faring even better, of course, what with his dry feet, which he kept reminding me of and which meant I might have to push him into a pond if we happened upon one. Thinking about it, I probably wouldn't even need to do that, as Rob is incredibly clumsy, and he would probably fall into one himself at some point along the way.

We followed the track straight through the farm, with a caged sheepdog loudly alerting everyone within around five miles to our presence. He didn't look too happy to see us, and I was glad there was wire between us and his teeth. Other noises emanated from within various barns, and I distinctly heard pigs and cows, presumably all stowed inside for the winter.

There was nobody else around as we left the farm behind us and entered a muddy field along a flooded track that was almost a river in places. The rain still fell all around us, though for a minute or two, we wondered if the sky was getting just a little brighter but then dismissed these thoughts as mere foolishness.

Following the edge of the field, we came across another information board, which once more told us all about the Pilgrimage of Grace. It was more or less the same board as last time, and the only difference was the photograph of the panorama before us, which labelled different hills and places due to the changed direction of the outlook, which now faced west.

Prominent on this one was Kilnwick Percy, which had not been visible from the first sign. Not that it was visible from this one, either, due to the low hanging cloud and the rain, but nevertheless, you could presumably see it on a clear day.

It told us that Thomas Heneage had owned Kilnwick Percy Hall at the time when Henry VIII was on the throne and that Heneage was, in fact, the king's secretary. This is not entirely accurate, and as we shall see, being on the throne in regard to this matter can be taken in the most literal sense.

Heneage, you see, was Henry VIII's *Groom of the Stool*. Not sure what that is? Well, basically, the official job description reads something like *the most intimate of the monarch's courtiers, responsible for assisting the king in excretion and hygiene.* He wiped the king's bum, then.

The job went by some other titles, such as the *valet of the chamber*, the *gentleman of the bedchamber*, or even the *servant of the long robe*. At some point, stool became stole, and when the throne was occupied by a woman, it became the *first lady of the bedchamber*. Regardless of whatever fancy job title the role had, however, the job still involved wiping bums, which may not sound all that appealing, but whoever did this job was about as close as you could get to a king or queen, which meant they held a lot of influence, which in turn meant they themselves became powerful individuals who commanded respect. But they still wiped bums. You'd never get that from a proper history book, would you?

After tramping through a few damp fields, we came to one with a beware of the bull sign. However, the only bull was the sign itself, as the field was empty. A quick hop across a main road had us in yet more damp fields, and while we had earlier thought that conditions could not get much worse, conditions got worse. We slid our way slowly along, trying to keep to the paths wherever possible, and all the while, I had my camera ready, just in case Rob went for that swim he was due.

A quick diversion around Wold Farm involved several ingenious water obstacles and a fair bit of hedge hopping, followed by yet more squishy fields, where Rob said that his feet were now also beginning to feel just a little bit wet. This had just been a matter of time, and while I would never gloat over such a turn of events, I did enjoy just a little smile, but only a tiny one, honest.

We were not far from Nunburnholme now, and the fields led us into a small wood and down a steep hill that had become a temporary waterfall due to the day's deluge. I suggested to Rob that we stop here if we could, hopefully in the church, where we could at least enjoy a few dry moments to eat our lunch.

Coming down through the wood, on a path that became alarmingly steep given the treacherous conditions underfoot, we could see the church off in the distance, prettily framed by trees on either side.

We trudged on in silence, and at the bottom of the hill, we met the road into the village, though our path would lead us across one last field and directly to the church. A lady had parked her car here, and she said hello to us as we passed. We stopped to talk to her, and she asked us where we were going on such a nice day. When we asked her where she was going, she just said she had come out for some fresh air, which was ironic, as she stood smoking a cigarette the whole time she was talking to us.

According to the map, the actual path followed the edges of the field, though everyone else seemed to have decided to go directly across the middle, judging by the small path that had been eroded away. Not wanting to be left out, we followed suit, and after just a few steps, we realised our mistake.

The ground underfoot became a sponge, and each step involved making your own temporary puddle and stepping straight into it. This was perhaps worse for Rob, as he weighed a hell of a lot more than me, so his puddles were twice the size of mine. He won't mind me saying that because it's true, and I'm not saying he's fat, but he is just a big guy, or as our friend Chris says, he's a big unit.

By the time we got to the other side of the field and emerged onto a narrow country road that was also waterlogged, it was probably fair to say that we were both suffering from the early signs of trench foot. Luckily, we were now just yards from the church, which meant we could at least get out of the rain for a while.

We wandered through the churchyard and round the back to the door, hoping it would be open, and I was thrilled when I felt the click of the handle and heard the creak of the door as it slowly opened.

The dimly lit interior beckoned us in nonetheless, and it was a relief when I took my hat off and allowed the air to flow around my soggy head. Rob dropped his backpack, and we both went to have a look around the church.

I had read that Nunburnholme had been more or less destroyed and abandoned following William the Conqueror's harrowing of the north, where he burned countless towns and villages and murdered a vast swathe of the population.

When people eventually returned, they built the village in a slightly different place, and this explained the church's current position on the edge of the village, rather than in the centre as would be expected.

St James was in good condition today, though, partly down to the fact that it was restored in the 1870s by famous architect George Gilbert Scott, who is perhaps better known for designing buildings such as The Albert Memorial in London, as well as the Midland Hotel, which is the really swanky looking hotel in front of St Pancras Station. Every time I have been past this hotel, the car park has always been full of Ferraris and Porsches and the like, which should give you an idea of the place.

Anyway, when they were restoring this church, they found an ancient cross, and although it was broken, they managed to fix it and even incorporated it into the church. It is now built into the base of the tower, but unfortunately, when they fixed it, they mounted the cross back to front.

It is worth a look, though, and features a rather interesting scene which tells the story of the legend of a Norse hero called Sigurd. After he killed a dragon called Fafnir, helped by his foster father Regin, Sigurd burnt his thumb while roasting the dragon's heart. It might not be a very impressive comparison, but I feel for Sigurd, as I once burnt my finger while cooking a chicken. Anyway, he then put his thumb in his mouth, as you might well do after burning it, I imagine, and inadvertently swallowed some of the dragon's blood. It is this that is said to have given him the ability to instantly understand the language of the birds, who told Sigurd that Regin was about to kill him. Regin, perhaps not surprisingly, is the one holding the sword.

Perhaps more interesting is the sheela-na-gig, and before I came here, I did not know what one of those was either. It was Rob who first noticed it, but then he was taller than me, and he called me over, giggling like a little schoolboy at his little discovery.

A sheela-na-gig, then, is basically a quasi-erotic carving of a woman and, as can be seen here, and I am sorry for this before I even say it, a woman that is pulling apart her vulva. This depiction, despite being overtly sexual, is also usually quite grotesque and sometimes even comical, and the one in Nunburnholme is somewhere between the two, in my opinion at least. Whichever way you look at it, then, this church is definitely worth a look.

We didn't want to eat in the church, so we went back outside and sat in the shelter of the porch. The rain was still coming down, but we managed to stay dry, though we only sat there for as long as it took us to eat, as it was not very warm at all.

It was with some reluctance, then, that we set off once again, back out into the rain and the cold, but we figured we only had around five miles or so left to go at the most. Unfortunately, the first thing we had to tackle was a rather steep hill which took us up onto Burnby Wold. A sign asked all visitors to stick to the path as soon as we left the village, but unfortunately, the path was blocked by a rather large tractor, so we swam around it and carried on.

The next obstacle was the ford at Nunburnholme Beck, which was probably and usually just a small stream, though today it was an impressive raging torrent that threatened to carry anyone away if you tried to cross it, even a giant such as Rob. Luckily, there was a small bridge just a few yards downstream hidden behind some bushes, and although I was tempted to let Rob wade through the river, at the last minute and just as he was about to step in, I just couldn't let him do it, so I told him about the bridge.

After this, it was uphill, and this was the most slippery bit of path we had come across so far, which was certainly saying something. A small fence ran alongside us to our left, and as I made my way up, I made use of it to make sure I didn't fall, and I only grabbed the barbed wire that topped the fence on one occasion. I thought I had cut myself, but it was just a scratch, although I still managed to use a couple of spicy words, so I was glad that nobody was around.

It took us ages to get up this hill, as we were

literally moving just one step at a time, and those steps were baby steps. Halfway up, we stumbled upon a grisly sight as we found a dead sheep behind a bush. While that may sound like a joke, it certainly wasn't. Rob said it was just asleep, or maybe it was resting its eyes, but it certainly didn't look like that to me.

We plodded on, and the path took us to the right and straight towards a scary-looking horse. He was munching whatever soggy grass he could find, and he was totally blocking our way. I'm not normally one to be scared of animals while I am out and about, but something about the way he stopped chewing his food and just stared at us made me uneasy. I did the only thing I could and made Rob go first.

I had to prod him once or twice with a sharp branch to make him move forwards, and as he neared the horse, its head slowly tracked and followed him, keeping a firm and beady eye on him. It didn't move, though, and made no attempt to murder him, so after a while, I slowly followed.

This stretch of path was even worse than the last, and I almost went over on more than one occasion. Successfully making it past the horse, the next obstacle was a gate surrounded by around a foot of water, but it was our only option.

After this, we slid along the path towards Partridge Hall, and it slowly became less waterlogged. The hall itself provided something of a track, which was a welcome relief, and after this, we were soon back on a road.

A sign told us it was just over a mile to Londesborough, which meant that it was probably around four to Market Weighton, and I think it is fair to say that we had both had enough of walking for the day. We had stopped talking by now, not for any reason other than we were cold, wet and miserable, and we plodded on in silence, moving aside only for the odd passing car.

The undulating road tortured us with yet more pointless ups and downs, and we saw another one of those little signs telling you what you could see in the distance. This was, apparently, the Vale of York, although once again, low cloud obscured any and all views for today. On a clearer day, the sign told us, you would see the delights of Doncaster, glorious Goole, and the magnificent Menwith Hill.

As we walked into the village of Londesborough, we could smell coal fires in the air. I asked Rob if he fancied a wander down Love Lane, but this just made him look very worried indeed. Love Lane, I explained, was simply the road to our left, but as he was clearly not all that keen, we carried straight on towards the church.

Londesborough is a small and rather pleasing little village. Some say that it is the location of the long-lost and still to be discovered Roman city Of Delgovicia, but as I haven't brought my spade with me today, I shall have to get back to you on that one. There is some evidence to support this, though, specifically the fact that a Roman road ran north from Brough, on the banks of the Humber estuary, and came straight to this place. Furthermore, Roman coins and other artifacts have all been found in this vicinity, so there may well be more down there than what is currently known.

On the grounds of Londesborough Park, there is a stately home called Londesborough Hall. The current one, dating from Victorian times, is nice, but the previous one, of Elizabethan origin, was on a grander scale altogether. That one had been built by George Clifford, the 3rd Earl of Cumberland, in 1589, but was demolished by a subsequent owner in 1839, one William Cavendish, the 6th Duke of Devonshire, to pay for repairs to his main house, which was Chatsworth House in Derbyshire.

I had come across Clifford before, when I had walked the Yorkshire Wolds Way with Rob and Chris, and it turns out that he was something of a character, although he did have something of a troubled life. His father died while he was very young, and his wardship was granted to the

Earl of Bedford, who happened to be Sir Francis Drake's godfather, a small fact that ultimately appears to have had a big effect on Clifford's later life. The Earl ultimately arranged for his daughter to marry Clifford, and, as arranged marriages tend to be, it was not a happy one.

I remembered that I had previously acquired the distinct impression that George Clifford may well have been the inspiration for Rowan Atkinson's comedic portrayal of Edmund Blackadder, the one from the second series of the programme set in Elizabethan times which is exactly the same time period that Cavendish lived in.

The similarities are many. Lord Blackadder served as a nobleman in the court of Elizabeth I, as did Clifford. Clifford was a gambler and a spendthrift, as was Blackadder, and both were highly intelligent, charismatic and handsome. Finally, Blackadder also spent a lot of time competing against the Queen's other courtiers, as did Clifford.

It was one of these other courtiers, the Marquess of Bath, who wrote to the Earl of Essex complaining about Clifford, and he clearly didn't like us uncultured northerners. He said of Clifford, and I quote, that he was *'the rudest Earl by reason of his northerly bringen up.'*

Clifford wasn't bothered what others thought

of him, though, and he embarked on many long and often dangerous expeditions to rob Spanish and Portuguese ships of whatever treasures they might be carrying. His career was long and successful, and he gained something of a reputation as a nautical Don Quixote, which is odd because Don Quixote was a gentleman, and the one thing that Clifford most certainly was not, was a gentleman. Faithless to his wife and with a temper like no other, while Clifford may not be quite as well-known as Sir Francis Drake, he was nonetheless just as successful when it came to robbing sailors and stealing booty. It's perhaps a shame then that all of the money he made from his time on the high seas was lost as he frittered it all away by gambling on horse racing and jousting.

Going back to Londesborough Hall, the decision to demolish it was said to be one that the 6th Duke of Devonshire ultimately regretted. Later on, he had a hunting box built on the estate, which was eventually enlarged and formed the basis of the Victorian hall that stands there today, but when he encountered financial problems in the 1840s, he sold it to the *Railway King* George Hudson.

Hudson didn't so much want the estate to live on but merely wanted to build a railway line through it and, at the same time, stop his rival George Leeman from also building railway lines through this area. Unfortunately, some of the shady practices employed by Hudson eventually ensured his own downfall, one of which was using company money to build his own private train station, which was exclusively for his own use. Eventually, he fled abroad in order to avoid debtors' prison, returning only when the law was changed, and debtors were no longer necessarily incarcerated.

The church was empty today and incredibly quiet, so we sat and rested for a while in utter silence, not really wanting to go back outside and into the elements. We did discover that the doorway of the church was built by the Normans shortly after their conquest of England, maybe as a way to show that they weren't all that bad after all, but eventually, we knew we had to move, and made our way through the village and into Londesborough Park.

The park was also empty today, not surprising considering the continuing rain. Even in this poor weather, however, this was a truly beautiful place, and it has been like this for hundreds of years.

The gardens were first laid out by Robert Hooke in the 1600s, which is surprising, as Hooke was primarily a scientist and architect and was a very busy man. He worked as an assistant to Christopher Wren and made a significant contribution to the rebuilding of

London after the great fire that ravaged the city in 1666, and he was also friends with Sir Isaac Newton early on in his career.

At some point, however, Hooke seems to have had a bit of a falling out with Newton. This falling out is probably why no portrait of Hooke exists today, although there definitely was a portrait of him at the Royal Society in his lifetime. After Hooke's death, you see, Newton became the president of the Royal Society, and the portrait of Hooke mysteriously vanished, never to be seen again.

Newton also made considerable efforts to paint Hooke as a miserable old curmudgeon, something which stuck for quite a while. However, when someone found and published Hooke's personal diaries in 1935, a completely different picture of Hooke began to emerge. He was actually a character that enjoyed the company of his friends in the coffee houses and taverns of old London, and he even recalls his secretive love affair with his very own niece, the filthy rascal. Furthermore, when someone discovered a stash of yet more of Hooke's papers at the Royal Society in 2006, this further portrayed him as a very happy sort indeed, and nothing like the picture painted by Newton.

Whatever the truth is, Londesborough is very nice indeed, and we should all be very grateful to Hooke for what he left us, and in particular, we should be grateful for the paths on a wet day such as today.

We followed these paths through the grounds of the former hall, and we soon passed a big oak tree that seemed to have found a way to stop itself from falling over. It was clearly leaning at a perilous angle, possibly due to soft soil or shallow roots, yet nevertheless, it somehow remained standing. Some of its branches had actually grown down towards the ground and were acting as some kind of prop or a hand to stop the tree from leaning further. How a tree could do this is beyond me, and maybe it was just chance, but as I said to Rob, it makes you think.

We left the hall behind and crossed a small lane, looking for a path that would lead us along Towthorpe Beck and finally into Market Weighton. It was easy enough to find, as we heard the gushing water of the small stream, which was totally overflowing today.

The fields had begun to flood, but both of us were beyond caring now, and we simply trudged through deep puddles that had once been a path. We were close to our final destination for the day, and we just wanted to finish, so we really didn't care about getting any wetter as this was clearly not possible. As we crossed a bridge over the bulging stream, the scene looked almost primordial. Beyond this was a small meadow of snowdrops that were just beginning to flower, though they were certainly at risk of being flooded if the water got any higher.

We trudged from field to field, trying not to slip and fall at this late hour, and it was with some relief when we finally hit the tarmac and found ourselves back where we had started, in Market Weighton. There was nothing to say as we made our way back to the car, other than next time, Rob suggested, perhaps we should bring some scuba gear and a life jacket.

The Birthplace Of Beer

Market Weighton to Beverley

Just a few days later, we somehow managed to find the time in our busy schedules to continue our walk. As we were getting nearer and nearer to our homes with every step, we were able to park the car in Beverley and take the bus back to Market Weighton, and in contrast to the last time we were up here, the sun was out, and there was not a single cloud to be seen in the sky. The weather gods were back, and I don't mean Neptune and Poseidon.

Spring had sprung, apparently, and the forecast promised several fine days ahead, during which, coupled with some free time, we both eagerly relished the thought of finishing this walk.

It had been a weird one, being so close to home, but it did at least help us realise that sometimes you ignore whatever was on your own doorstep. We had passed through places and villages that we not only had never previously visited but we never even knew existed. Beautiful woods and winding lanes, pleasant pubs and parks, and lots more besides, all on our own doorstep. We should do this more often, I said to Rob.

The ride to Market Weighton was short and functional. The bus was packed to the rafters with old codgers, all happily getting the most from their free bus passes probably, but then can you really blame them? If I had one, I'd be using it too, and on top of that, if it means that there aren't lots of Sunday drivers dithering along the road in front of me, all cruising steadily along at a snail's pace and forming huge backlogs of traffic, that's got to be a good thing, surely?

And before you have a go about me picking on the pensioners, there is a reason that you have to re-take your driving test at a certain age, and that is because most of us start to lose certain faculties as we get older. And we all get more and more cautious as we get older too, which means that the carefree teenager who, once upon a time, would happily pull out in front of a speeding juggernaut, ignoring all risk to life and limb while slipping said thunder-trucker the middle finger, would eventually turn into an old fart who will quite happily sit at a junction waiting for that tractor he or she has just seen about a mile distant, while they discuss the effects of ladybirds on marigolds and daffodils with their passengers, all while simultaneously trying to tune the car stereo into Radio Four.

Yes, it's definitely better for all mankind that they are packed nicely onto this bus, thereby freeing the roads up for us lesser mortals and reckless daredevils, and to hell with the thunder trucks.

We almost missed our stop in Market Weighton, though, as Rob and I were, in fact, discussing the effects of ladybirds on marigolds and daffodils, but there you go. Luckily, around a thousand years' worth of old people decided to get off, which aroused us from our exciting debate on insects, and we waited patiently for them all to shuffle off before us, but it was okay as they only took around three hours to clear the bus. They then decided, very kindly and en masse, to all stand and chat at the bus stop, thereby blocking the way for Rob and myself, and as we excused ourselves and tried to make our way through the crowd, Rob inadvertently took at least two of them out with his rucksack. I told him it was okay that he probably killed a couple of them, as they would not have had much time left to spend on this planet anyway, and he told me something that I already knew, which was the fact that I am a very disturbed human being. I thanked him for his kindness, and we moved on.

Immediately, we encountered something very rare indeed, as we came across someone that was even bigger than Rob. I know I have mentioned this before, but he really is very tall, at least compared to a midget such as myself, and it is not often that we meet people that are bigger than him.

Technically, however, we never met that actual person, but we did come across a statue of him, with him being William Bradley, more commonly known as the Yorkshire Giant. I pondered whether or not Market Weighton was a poor place, though, as the statue of Bradley was not made of bronze or stone, as most tend to be, but was made of wood. Don't get me wrong, it was very nice, and assuming it was to scale, Bradley certainly was a very tall guy indeed. But wood? Really?

Anyway, Bradley was born and bred here, presumably surprising his parents when he popped out in February 1787 as he was already rather large, weighing a whopping 14 pounds. When I mentioned this to my wife, it understandably made her eyes water, and she told me that this would be like giving birth to a four-month-old. I can remember what my kids were like when they were that age, and let's just say they were chubby little bunnies, certainly not something I would want to pass or be able to, for that matter.

Anyway, Bradley quickly grew and was soon far bigger than any of the other children at his school. It is said that people made fun of him, which was perhaps not the best idea, as he used to pick his fellow pupils up and place them on the beams of the ceiling high above even his own head, and would only take them down when instructed to do so by his teachers, who actually became complicit in his mischief and used Bradley as a way to make the kids behave. You couldn't get away with this now, of course, what with human rights and child abuse laws, though I bet it was effective at the time.

Perhaps not surprisingly, Bradley eventually found himself as part of a freak show, where he was described as England's tallest man. He made a modest living from his height and even met the king at some point. The king gave Bradley an oversized pocket watch, which he was clearly very proud of and which he wore for the rest of his life.

Unfortunately, the rest of his life was not all that long. Bradley died at the relatively young age of 33, probably from complications relating to his size. In fact, many over-sized people die quite young, and although there are many reasons for this and not simply one factor, some things are very clear. For instance, each additional 4 inches of height increases your risk of all types of cancer by 13 percent, which is pretty scary when you think about it. And furthermore, taller people have higher levels of growth hormone and insulin, both of which have been found to promote chronic diseases and reduced longevity, which does not sound all that good, does it? I'm glad I'm a midget, I told my giant friend Rob, through what can only be described as an evil smile.

Bradley was buried locally, originally in the graveyard, but his body was quickly moved into the church due to fears that grave robbers would attempt to steal his body. This was a real thing then, and theft of bodies was quite common and was referred to at the time as body-snatching, with the culprits referred to as resurrection men and with the bodies usually sold to doctors for medical research or dissection.

Perhaps the most famous of these resurrection men were William Burke and William Hare, more commonly known as simply Burke and Hare, who famously graduated from selling already dead bodies to actual murder. They ultimately sold sixteen of their victims to an Edinburgh doctor called Robert Knox, who dissected bodies on a daily basis in front of hundreds of aspiring medical professionals and any other weirdos who cared to watch and who therefore had a desperate and ongoing need for cadavers. It is worth noting that Burke and Hare had initially tried to sell their victims to a professor called Alexander Monro, but they were instead directed to Knox, with whom they eventually came to an understanding.

Obviously, you can't go around topping people off and chopping them up and expect to get away with it forever. Burke and Hare were eventually caught and put on trial, although Hare made a deal, provided a full confession, and was thus exempted from prosecution. Burke, therefore, took the full blame for the murders and was convicted and hanged. Quite fittingly, perhaps, his body was donated to medical science, and he suffered the same fate as that of his victims and was thoroughly and generously dissected after his death, with hundreds of people coming to view the spectacle.

And with some irony, it was Professor Monro who dissected Burke's body, and he certainly seemed to have enjoyed what he did, judging by his actions. During the dissection, you see, Monro dipped the quill of his pen into Burke's blood and wrote, *'This is written with the blood of Wm Burke, who was hanged at Edinburgh. This blood was taken from his head.'* I can only assume that perhaps Monro was still drunk from the night before, but who knows. Furthermore, it is said that a book was bound with some of

Burke's own skin, which, along with his skeleton, can still be found on the dusty shelves of an Edinburgh museum, I told Rob.

We had gone off on a bit of a tangent, and it was time to come back to Market Weighton, so we wandered a few yards to have a look at William Bradley's house, which stood just a short walk away from his statue. Not surprisingly, the house was built to unusual proportions, with the ceilings being somewhat higher than your average house, and the doorways were, well, huge, but then they would have to be, wouldn't they?

For a small town, Market Weighton has another interesting little tale to tell. We found out about this next one on a previous visit when we wandered up the high street and discovered one of those blue plaques that often mark historical locations or perhaps the homes of notable residents. This particular one related to Hilda Lyon, and while she might not be that well known, she is very famous in engineering circles, as it was Hilda that came up with something called the Lyon shape, which, to put it simply, is the most aerodynamically efficient shape that an airship can be. Later on, this technology also became quite important for submarines, and it is amazing to think that it all started here, with Hilda Lyon.

It was time to leave this pleasant little town,

though, and after stocking up on food at a small baker's shop, we headed north towards the disused railway line. We found it soon enough after wandering through a small housing estate and passing by a deserted children's park, presumably empty because all of the little monsters were safely locked away in one school or another.

There were some girls playing football on the field behind the park, though, presumably part of a school team, and I told Rob that if they had been doing this a few years ago, they would have been in trouble. He looked puzzled, so I went on to explain that the Football Association had actually banned women's football in 1921, basically because it was getting a bit too popular for them to cope with, which is truly astounding when you think about it.

Women were therefore barred from using any grounds, equipment or facilities belonging to any club that was a member of the association, which was essentially all of them in reality. Instead, women were forced to play on scrubland, parks and private gardens, or basically, anywhere they could, just so long as they didn't play on an actual football pitch. We would consider this crazy nowadays, but what is even crazier is that this ban wasn't lifted until 1971.

Moving on, the transformation from street

to farmer's field was more or less instant. One minute we were in a bustling little market town with traffic and shoppers and noise and everything else you might expect, and the next, we were in among the trees with birds singing all around us and with sheep munching silently away in the next field.

The sun was still out and had risen a little higher in the sky, and whatever chill had been in the air had now most definitely vanished. Today was a very good day indeed.

Rob and I wandered along the straight and level path, which was obviously well maintained, and chatted about this and that, and we almost missed the turn that would take us up to Goodmanham.

Seeing it at the last minute, we darted left and made our way across a field and towards the village, which was clearly visible just a few hundred yards in front of us. We seemed to be following another disused railway line for a few yards, and when I later checked, I discovered that it was indeed an old trackbed and had once taken passengers and goods from here to Driffield.

A suspiciously new-looking windmill stood attached to a house near the beginning of the village, and we discussed whether or not it was original. It looked really good, too good, to be honest, but it was still very nice.

We stopped momentarily, and I filled up my water bottle in the crystal-clear stream that ran under a bridge next to the mill. The water around here is always good for drinking, but don't take my word for it, as I don't want anyone blaming me if they get a bad case of the plague or maybe something even worse. Anyway, my bottle has a built-in filter and is one of the best investments I have made when it comes to walking gear and equipment. When you think about it, water is probably the heaviest thing you carry when you go for a walk, and having a filter means not having to carry so much. It is not so much an issue on short walks such as this one, but whenever I have done multi-day walks, it is very noticeable when you have three litres of extra weight on your back in the form of water. And being blessed as we are by living on an island that is literally covered with the stuff, and when much of the time it is falling from the sky, a water filter makes perfect sense.

Thinking of this makes me wonder how on earth we still manage to have water shortages every summer. In fact, droughts often follow floods, which is surely purely and simply mismanagement, but who am I to say? I merely studied politics and economics. Anyway, this reminds me of one of the most memorable quotes ever made in this country by a politician about politicians, in my mind at least. In 1945, just after the end of the Second World War when the country was suffering from a shortage of food and energy, the deputy leader of the Labour Party, Aneurin Bevan, better known as Nye Bevan, said this little plumb of a sentence:

'This island is made mainly of coal and surrounded by fish. Only an organisational genius could produce a shortage of both coal and fish at the same time.'

He was right, as the government of the day had well and truly cocked up, although, in fairness, they had been somewhat distracted by a moustachioed Austrian for the last few years, for we really should remember that Adolf Hitler was actually born in Austria and not Germany. I know we've gone somewhat off-topic again, but please get used to it, as I do it all the time, but it's always something of interest, I promise. Regardless of all of this, surely the same principle applies to our water, and it can only be, as I have already said, mismanagement?

Anyway, the stop was worth it, too, as the water tasted fresh and cold and was very refreshing indeed. It did have a distinctive taste, though, due to the chalk that is found throughout these hills, but it was nice nonetheless.

We made our way up into the village, passing several nice houses along the way. Fields to our right housed numerous calves, none of which took any notice of us, too busy as they were mowing the lawn, so to speak.

It was a bit of an uphill walk, so we were happy to stop at the top and take advantage of a picnic table outside the pub for a few minutes. The pub was the Goodmanham Arms, and although it was firmly closed at this early hour, it is a very nice place indeed and one I have been to on many occasions.

In fact, the last time I was here, someone had mistaken me for someone famous, although I never found out who. Regardless, the free round of drinks had gone down very nicely. And every time I have been in, the staff have always been very friendly, and they seem to enjoy running the place.

The interior is very nice too, all olde-worlde, with axes and swords hanging from the walls, which might make it interesting on a Saturday night. Well, it would be where I am from.

We carried on, and I told Rob what I knew about Goodmanham, which was a fair bit. We had walked through here a few years previously, as the Yorkshire Wolds Way also passes through the village, and it is a place with a lot of history.

Goodmanham, I reminded Rob, was the ancient home of the Parisii tribe, who built their chief temple here, making it the holiest place in the ancient Kingdom of Northumbria. This temple was the *Great Temple of Woden*, with Woden being the father of the gods, apparently, although it was also called the *Great Temple of the Idols*. Whatever it was called, it stood here for hundreds of years, until 627 AD that is, when King Edwin renounced Paganism in favour of Christianity.

The story goes that his high priest, who went by the name of Coifi, rode up here on a horse from York, threw an axe or a spear at the door of the temple, and then set fire to it and burned it down to the ground, which reminded me of a night out in Newcastle a few years back. Anyway, on a serious note, this was all meant to be a symbolic act to demonstrate the abandoning of the old ways in favour of the new.

The fact that Coifi did this is odd in itself, as he was specifically barred from either riding horses or carrying weapons, as were all holy men, so we can perhaps take his act as his final defiance against Paganism itself. Anyway, with this action, the Kingdom of Northumbria, which stretched from the Humber all the way up to the Firth of Forth in Scotland and as far west as the Isle of Man, was converted to Christianity in a single stroke.

Coifi may not have ridden from York, though. Another legend tells us that he came here from Londesborough, which we recently passed through, of course, as this was where the royal camp was based in the summer months, but the truth is not really known for sure.

There is probably some truth in there somewhere, however, as this story was told by none other than St Bede, also known as the Venerable Bede, who was said to be the father of English history. And the church that stands before us today was built on the site of the original temple and is itself somewhat ancient, dating back over 800 years.

But what caused Edwin to turn to Christianity? Well, guess what? It was a woman.

He had formed an alliance with the powerful kingdom of Kent and cemented it by marrying Princess Ethelburga, who was the daughter of the King, Ethelberht. However, Ethelburga was already a Christian and only agreed to the marriage if she could bring her Priest, Paulinus, with her to the frozen north.

Edwin agreed, and after a couple of years of marriage, he held a conference, probably at Londesborough, to decide which religion everyone should follow. He asked Paulinus to put the case for Christianity and Coifi to put the case for Paganism. Surprisingly, Coifi was not at all interested in defending Paganism, which at least helps to explain why he then grabbed a horse and a pointy thing as well as some matches and then did what he did in Goodmanham. In summary, then, it was here that England officially adopted Christianity, which is certainly quite a big claim to fame, it has to be said, so I'm surprised they don't make more of it, to be honest.

We wandered into the church for a moment, just for a nosey really, where I was delighted to find stained glass windows depicting all of the main characters in this story. This included Edwin, Ethelburga and Paulinus, as well as Bede, of course, but best of all is the image of Coifi, who is holding a flaming torch, being the pyromaniac that he was, and he also had a rather dapper sword at his side.

We didn't stay long, as we wanted to get some miles under our feet, and we were soon on the road out of the village that took us back towards the disused railway line. Coming into Goodmanham had been a bit of a diversion from the railway line, and although it was a welcome one, there is something interesting to see for anyone who skips Goodmanham and stays on the track, and that would be St Helen's Well.

The well is well worth a visit, if you pardon the pun, and is perhaps a good place to refill your water bottles. I always fill mine up when passing by, and I haven't been poisoned yet, and the water is about as fresh as you can get, popping out of the side of a hill as it does. It has been well filtered by the chalk, and in my opinion, it is very nice to drink, although, in this day and age of health and safety madness, I did remember seeing a sign on my last visit advising passers-by not to drink water from the well. All I can say is that I like to fly by the seat of my pants, and I drink the stuff anyway, being the reckless old rock and roller that I am. Anyway, where do you think mineral water comes from?

In centuries gone by, the well was said to have been used as a place of healing, possibly in the odd-shaped bath that can still be seen today, and later on, it was used as a source of water for any passing steam engines that were perhaps themselves a little bit thirsty too.

More recently, locals and visitors have taken to tying ribbons and flowers onto tree branches around the well, probably as a way to remember loved ones but also maybe for good luck. Obviously, the interfering types that don't want us to drink the water also don't want us to tie stuff into the trees, and there was a sign there saying that on my last visit. However, judging by the brightly coloured decorations hanging from many branches around the well, not many people take any notice of that either, and I don't blame them one bit.

Anyway, who was St Helen? Well, you're going to like this, as we have, in fact, already come across her on the first day of our journey. Cast your mind back to the very start of our walk, and when I say the very start, I mean it in the most literal sense. If you remember when we were standing outside of the minster in York, and we came across Constantine the Great, we discovered that his mum, Helena, had been the one who had wandered around the middle east, finding such things as the true cross of Christ and bags of nails and all of that. Well, Constantine's mum, Helena, is in fact, St Helen. She is also known as St Eleanor and Helen of Constantinople because, let's face it, you can't have too many names, can you?

Anyway, this is her well, and very nice it is, too, although it is not nice enough to make us walk the half a mile or so back towards Market Weighton, so instead, we carried on towards the east. Interestingly, Goodmanham also has a couple of other wells, namely Lady's Well and Beggar's Bush Well, which, although they are both not bad names, both of the actual wells are just a bit disappointing, being nothing more than muddy, wet holes in the ground, and neither is a match for St Helen's Well, so we moved on.

The good thing about walking along disused railway lines is that they are generally fairly flat. The bad thing about walking along disused railway lines is also that they are fairly flat. While it makes for easy walking, for the next half a mile or so, we were contained within a rather boring valley, with not a lot to see.

Yes, it was nice enough, with fields and trees and cowpats and all that country stuff, but it was just, well, dull. There were no animals darting in front of us, no people to speak to, and although the sun was out and it was nice enough, as I have already said, it was just, well, flat.

All of this went out of the window, however, when I heard someone shouting behind me, and I knew instantly that we were in for a good time. Rob's eyes lit up, too, as we saw the source of the noise.

Around a hundred yards behind us, we spied two people, a male and a female. As they caught us up, the man said something rather surprising to us, and it is something which I cannot possibly put down in writing, but I can say it began with the sixth letter of the alphabet and ended in 'uckers'. I looked at Rob, and he looked at me, and although we did not quite know how to react, when he immediately repeated his favourite word, we both burst out laughing.

The lady apologised and said she was his carer, all the while with him calling us a pair of, well, you know what. Perhaps he knew us, I suggested to Rob.

We walked with them for a bit, and we discovered that our new best friend was called Richard and that he liked walking, ice cream, small dogs, and swearing, and sometimes all of these things at once. His carer, who was called Jenny, also liked walking and dogs but did not seem all that keen on swearing, which was a shame as I suggested she would probably be very good at it. She did, however, profess a great love for ice cream.

We tried not to encourage him, though it didn't seem to matter, and for the next mile or so, all I can say is that he made a very boring valley possibly the most interesting walk we had done so far this year.

It was a shame then when we bade them farewell, and as they continued along the railway line, we turned off and went into a nature reserve at Kiplingcoates. We had intended to find a picnic table and stop for lunch, but there was not a single one to be seen.

I wandered up a hill following a small path just in case there was anything beyond the horizon while Rob waited at the bottom. I found nothing, so we returned the way we had come in, as it did not look like there was a way back to the trail further on, and we did not want to walk to the other end of the reserve just to have to walk back again.

If Kiplingcotes sounds familiar, then it may be because you have heard of the Kiplingcotes Derby, possibly the oldest horse race in the world. It was first run in 1519 and has been held more or less every year since. I say more or less because although it has technically been run every year, in some of those years, there has only been one entrant allowed. This is because of a rule that says if the race is ever not run for a year, then it must never be run again, so significant efforts have been made to keep the race alive.

In 1947, for instance, a harsh winter made the race more or less impossible, and in 2001, foot and mouth disease saw vast swathes of the English countryside closed to more or less everyone and everything. More recently, 2018 saw flooding disrupt the race, and even more recently, 2020 and 2021 once again saw solitary riders escorted around the route just to preserve the existence of the race for future generations, and I really hope I don't have to explain why this happened in those particular years.

While all this may sound a bit odd, there are some things to be said about the race that are even more strange. For instance, anyone can enter, and if you fancy having a go yourself, then you just need to turn up on the day and pay the entrance fee. However, you must weigh at least ten-stone, and if you are lucky enough to be lighter than this, you will have to weigh yourself down until you are heavy enough, either that or eat lots of biscuits beforehand.

And perhaps the oddest thing about the

race is the fact that the winner receives fifty pounds, with the rest of the prize money going to whoever comes in second place. In reality, this means that the runner up generally always receives more prize money than the winner, which begs the question, what is the bloody point in winning?

It must be prestige, suggests Rob, and he is right, and it is exactly this that is behind the fact that lots of people enter with ex-professional or retired racehorses, which is not strictly allowed. They will often change the name of the horse in order to be able to enter, which is an extreme length to go to, in my opinion anyway, but again, what do I know?

We wandered on, and the track began to gradually take us to the right, and off into the distance, we saw some buildings which looked like they were on the course of the railway line, probably an old train station.

We were right, and a few moments later, we arrived at Kiplingcotes station and found some rather nice picnic benches. The station was built by Lord Hotham, or more accurately, was built because of him, as it was Hotham who owned most of the land between Beverley and Market Weighton at the time. The fact that it was built at all was surprising, as although the line from York to Market Weighton had opened in 1847, it took another seventeen years for this section to open, and in fact, it nearly never happened at all. This was because Hotham initially refused permission for the line to cross his land, and he only relented when the railway company promised to build him his own personal station, which was this one, and also promised not to run trains on Sundays so as not to disturb the precocious Lord on the sabbath, and by the Lord, I mean Hotham, not God.

As a double bonus, we also found Richard and his carer here, busy having their lunch, so we said hello and plonked ourselves down at the table next to them, eager to be entertained.

Richard was clearly pleased to see us and once again began calling us some rather colourful names. This at least brightened up our short stop for lunch considerably, and I could not think of a better way to while away the day than to take in some sunshine and listen to lots of rather creative expletives.

To top it all off, Richard did probably the loudest and longest burp I have ever heard, which caused great amusement at our table, and Rob and I thought it only polite to return the gesture. Richard loved this and almost collapsed on the floor laughing, but Jenny did not look too impressed. We apologised for encouraging him, but she said it was fine and it was nice to see him laughing, and she also said something rather sad, which was that people often ignore him and fail to interact with him when he is out and about, which I can relate to, as I have experience of a similar situation myself. When my young son was ill with cancer, and after he had lost his hair and was wheelchair-bound, people I knew would actually cross the road so they didn't have to talk to us. I'm not angry or bitter about this, though, as I know full well why they did it. It wasn't that they didn't want to talk to us; they just didn't know what to say.

So don't get me wrong, I fully understand why some people are scared to talk to others, particularly those with a disability, but there is literally no difference between any of us, and at the end of the day, we all laugh at exactly the same things. But especially at swearing and burping. And farts.

We left them behind here, as they were heading back towards Market Weighton and we were carrying on towards Beverley, so we once again had the track to ourselves for a while.

Before we left the station, however, I went to look in an old signal box, which looked remarkably well preserved. I put my head against the window and peered into the dark interior, and it looked as if someone had turned it into an art studio. An easel stood in one corner, along with a table covered in too many pots of paint to count, and some rather nice pictures decorated the walls. It dawned on me that this was someone's private space, so I quickly left, and we wandered on, continuing our journey.

Rob hadn't tripped over yet, I reminded him, and he said he was having a day off. To be honest, the flat path made for a good walking surface, and the likelihood of a trip or a fall was minimal, which was good news for my clumsy friend.

I should probably mention that we were on this walk due to a sort of accident, as the Wilberforce Way was not meant to be our next adventure. When we had finished the Herriot Way some weeks before, we had decided that we would next tackle the Inn Way, an interesting sounding walk marketed with the tag line *90 miles, 7 days, 44 pubs*.

However, that walk would be one we would have to do all at once, and we had been unable to find a date near enough in the future, so we had decided to walk the Wilberforce Way instead, and I am glad we had. We often neglect what is on our own doorstep, as I may have already mentioned, and already on this footpath, we had discovered more interesting places than we could possibly have imagined. I had thought I knew my own backyard pretty well, but this walk was definitely proving me wrong, but in a good way.

The path meandered on, snaking slowly through the rolling hills of the Yorkshire Wolds, and as we were near a car park, we bumped into one or two people over the next couple of miles. A jogger took us by surprise from behind, and a cyclist passed us twice, first from the front and then also from behind, and I am not sure how far he had gone, but you can certainly cover a lot more miles on two wheels than you can on foot.

Presently, we came to a road, which meant we would be leaving the track for a while. The route of the walk took us away from the disused railway line for the next few miles, and it was a welcome distraction, as although the track was straight and flat, it had become somewhat monotonous, so left we went, heading towards Etton.

This tiny village has a rather unusual claim to fame. It was the birthplace and home of a man called Thomas Carling, who went on to found the massive and rather successful multinational brewing company that now bears his name. Unfortunately, he didn't build his empire here but moved to London in 1818. Not London, England, either, but London, Ontario, which is across the pond in deepest, darkest Canada. And, if I may get my home city in once again, he left via Hull, travelling by ship.

Once settled in Canada, he originally tried farming but also developed a small business brewing beer for the British soldiers garrisoned near his home, which proved to be very popular and much more successful than his farm. I must add that he took his recipe with him to Canada and that it was actually a traditional Yorkshire recipe for brewing beer which, therefore, later took over the world, even if it does taste like stale mole piss. I should probably apologise for saying that, and for legal reasons, I should probably say that it doesn't taste like stale mole piss at all. It actually tastes like badger juice. Make of that what you will. Anyway, it's cheaper than other beers for a reason, that's all I'm saying, and lastly, I'm more of a real ale fan, so I tend to avoid lagers, as does Rob. However, I will happily drink it if it's free and will quite willingly throw my principles completely out of the window every time there's a special offer on.

Rob reckoned that Carling gives you hangovers, but I disagreed and told him that I'd often had over ten pints of the stuff on a rowdy Saturday night out and other than the fact that it felt as if Lucifer himself was trying to crush my head in a vice, and the frequent urge to vomit up an acrid, green gunk that had the consistency of used cooking oil mixed with out-of-date milk, I had felt absolutely fine the next day. Admittedly, I did have a tattoo that had mysteriously appeared out of nowhere, and I had absolutely no idea who Santiago was or why his name was, well, down there.

Anyway, Carling started out with just two

kettles, and he sold his beer from a wheelbarrow on the streets of London. As his company expanded, he eventually built a six-storey brewery, which unfortunately burned down after just a year, but despite this and other setbacks, he never ever gave up.

Unfortunately, Thomas actually died of pneumonia just after the fire, probably due to the long-term effects of smoke inhalation. His family took over the business and later expanded the company throughout Canada, America, Europe and beyond, and don't infer anything in this, but as Carling expanded, the British Empire shrunk. Just saying.

Not a lot else ever happened in Etton, other than the fact that it also gave us at least one other person who also became quite significant in their lifetime, though not, unfortunately, by brewing beer. This other person was John Lothropp, better known as the Reverend John Lothropp.

Much like Carling, Lothropp also left Etton behind, though he was merely seeking religious freedom and had no wish to build a multi-national business empire. He had been arrested early in his career due to refusing to swear allegiance to the established church, and while it is not known if Lothropp himself was actually thrown in prison, several of his colleagues were locked in *The Clink*, which was actually a real prison in the London borough of Southwark, and is thus where the slang name for a jail originally came from.

Anyway, having had enough of constant persecution, Lothropp left England, also bound for America, and it is said that when he got there, he is said to have rejoiced in finding *a church without a bishop and a state without a king*. What Lothropp really became famous for, however, was his idea of the separation of church and state, a principle that went on to underpin the foundations of the United States and many other countries besides, so once again, world, you're welcome, as you basically have Yorkshire to thank for your freedom.

He ultimately lived a very prosperous life in his new country, although there wasn't much to do there, apparently, judging by the fact that he had thirteen children between his first and second wives. Not surprisingly, he has rather a lot of descendants, some reckon around 80,000, and the list of them reads like some kind of conspiracy theory. They range from U.S. presidents including Ulysses S Grant, Theodore Roosevelt and both George Bush Senior as well as George Bush Junior, followed by legendary gunfighter Wild Bill Hickock, financier and gazillionaire J.P. Morgan, not to mention Shirley Temple, Brooke Shields, Jake Gyllenhaal, Clint Eastwood and Kevin Bacon, along with much of America, apparently, if that list is anything to go by. And to think, it all started right here, in sleepy old Etton.

Today the village is deserted, apart from two rather suspicious-looking men with backpacks, of course. A road sign welcomed careful drivers but failed to mention reckless walkers, so we plodded on regardless.

Most of the village, in fact, all of the village, appeared to be on our left and consisted of some very nice houses and some equally nice street lights. They were not the modern type so often seen everywhere else but were of the Victorian type that looked really nice on Christmas cards.

At first, the houses were more modern, but in the centre of the village, we found the older ones, many of which had incredibly well-kept gardens. We were beginning to think that the place consisted solely of houses and nothing but houses, but then we eventually found a pub called The Light Dragoon, which presumably sold Carling.

Unfortunately, however, when we wandered over for a closer look and perhaps to pay it a visit and support that local economy, it became quite apparent that the pub was not only closed but appeared to be closed for good. This was a shame, but we did find a small plaque dedicated to Thomas Carling on a cottage directly opposite the pub, which told the family's story, and which also told us that John Carling, son of Thomas, was knighted by Queen Victoria in 1893 for services to either Canada or beer or Yorkshire, or perhaps all three. The queen, you see, quite liked her beer, as did her servants, who each managed to drink around eight pints of the stuff every day, so it must have been an interesting place to work, what with everyone, including the queen, being more or less constantly wasted.

We turned right just after the pub, passing possibly the most ornate war memorial we had ever seen, on a road which led us south and up a long but shallow hill. We edged cautiously along the side of the road as a group of lycra-clad cyclists passed us, who seemed to be going for the land speed record, apparently. I am always amazed at how fast they can go, and as each one passed us, we heard a rather impressive whoosh of air.

As the road levelled out, we were treated to the delights of a field full of deer, who were far enough away from us not to be afraid. Above them, a sparrowhawk circled in the air, and I guessed it was a male due to its bluish-grey back and wings. Females tend to be more of a brown colour and are also larger than males, which is a fact that is true across most birds of prey, surprisingly.

A couple of undulating hills led us south and towards Cherry Burton, and a road bridge took us over the railway line that had formed so much of today's walk. A couple of horseback riders were making their way down a track, so we stopped to talk to them for a minute, and they told us they had come from the farm just ahead of us and were taking their horses out for their daily exercise. I have a dog, and it can be quite demanding looking after her, so I can only imagine how hard it is to take care of a horse.

They asked us how far we had come, and they seemed somewhat alarmed when we said Market Weighton, which was several miles behind us by now. I am always surprised when people react like this, as walking ten, fifteen or sometimes twenty miles a day is no major feat of physical endurance. Over the years, I have come to the conclusion that most people simply assume they are not capable of walking such distances when in fact, they are. My philosophy is that the more you try it, the more you will be able to do it.

We carried on, with the road taking more ups and downs, and eventually, it brought us into the village of Cherry Burton itself. We stopped for a moment to sit down at a small feature that bore the name of the village, but it was only so Rob could take a stone out of his shoe, and I joked about how it had taken him so long to remove it, considering I had put it in there first thing this morning. For a minute, he didn't know whether or not to take me seriously, but then he realised I was just being me, and I am, in fact, an idiot who takes nothing seriously.

We passed many modern houses, which seemed to have their origins in the 1960s or possibly the 1970s, and we could have been anywhere in the country, but the village centre was much more pleasant, and no one shouted naughty words at us.

I even found a bookmark on the floor close to the phone box, which was now actually the village library, and I decided to recycle it and take it home with me, as a bookmark is not something I actually own. I do apologise if it was yours, but anyway, finders' keepers. What is it that they say? One man's trash is another man's treasure. Wonderful saying, but a horrible way to find out that you were adopted, I imagine.

We popped into the church just for a quick look and found some rather nice stained-glass windows, one of which was dedicated to someone called Captain Cecil Fowler Burton, who died of enteric fever in India. I didn't know what enteric fever was, but Rob told me it was typhoid and that the death from it was not a pleasant one at all, apparently. Still, the window was very pretty.

That there is a window here remembering Cecil is probably because his dad, David, owned Cherry Burton Hall, which is probably the biggest house in the village. Presumably, the family name derived from the village too, which was previously called North Burton, with the neighbouring village of Bishop Burton being referred to as South Burton once upon a time. In fact, there were once eight villages around here that used the name Burton, which must have been a bit confusing for the postie.

The church was supposedly consecrated by St John of Beverley, who was also said to have performed a miracle whilst here, but more of him later. What I did notice were lots of memorials to men who had died in one war or another.

The first one remembered a man called Robert Stickney who lived at nearby Gardham Hall, suggesting he was perhaps rather rich, of course. On the same plaque, a somewhat sad story unfolded, telling of how the Stickney family lost not only their son but also their son-in-law in the space of just a few tragic months during some of the darkest days of the Second World War. Perhaps curiously, however, the plaque made no reference to Robert Stickney's wife, which I found rather odd, to be honest.

Anyway, their son, Crichton Stickney, was the first to die. He was an officer in the Royal Air Force, and the 6th of July 1941 was to be the first fateful day for the family. Crichton had been piloting a Bristol Blenheim medium bomber, which was perhaps the mainstay of the RAF at the start of the war. There were over a thousand of them in service, and Winston Churchill paid homage to the bravery of their crews, comparing them to *The Charge of the Light Brigade*.

Stickney and his crew took off from RAF Wattisham in Suffolk, bound for a bombing mission over Nordeney, which was a German island in the North Sea. Not a great deal is known about the exact circumstances, but we do know that Stickney and his crew had been performing a low-level bombing run on an enemy ship. Unfortunately, they flew so low that they hit the ship's mast, causing the aircraft to crash into the sea with the loss of all on board. Stickney was just twenty years old.

Just a couple of months later, the family suffered a second tragedy with the loss of their son in law, Russell Welland, and perhaps rather cruelly, it occurred in strikingly similar circumstances.

Welland had been based in the middle east, and on the 12th of September 1941, he and his crew took off from Beirut in the Lebanon, heading to an area just west of the Suez Canal in Egypt. They were on an anti-submarine sweep of the area, so they would once again have been flying at an extremely low altitude, and they were also flying in a Bristol Blenheim.

All went well initially, and after just a couple of hours and with their mission completed, the crew signalled their intention to return to base and even ordered four late breakfasts. Unfortunately, nothing was ever heard of them again, and despite searches involving several aircraft, no trace was ever found of them or their plane. Welland had been just twenty-nine years old.

There were several other plaques that all told equally sad stories, and the only nice thing about them, perhaps, is that they were all really well cared for.

We didn't stay too long, and we were soon on our way again, making our way through the village, as we had seen everything there was to be seen. We had popped into the local shop for some snacks and wandered past the village pond, and we also passed Cherry Burton Hall just before we left the village completely. You couldn't see much of the house, though, as someone had built their own version of the Berlin Wall all around it, but what you could see was nice enough.

We would have popped into the pub, too, consistent with our habit of supporting the local economy, of course, but once again, we had managed to pass through on one of the few days when it was not open, which was a shame.

Still, we pressed on, under a still cloudless sky, and we reckoned we only had an hour or two to go before we got to Beverley, where we would be absolutely sure to find a way to support the local economy, I promised Rob.

The path took us out of the village along a twisting street and straight across a main road where I almost became the front bumper decoration for a bus, which seemed to be becoming something of a theme for this walk, it has to be said. Undaunted, we carried on, passing a rather nice-looking holiday park, before arriving at a small hump bridge where we would be able to re-join the disused railway line. For one minute, I thought we would have to fight our way through some bushes, but then Rob noticed some narrow steps on our left, which I had completely missed. I should probably book an eye test, I said, before Rob had the chance to.

We hopped down these steps and found ourselves back on the deserted track, safe from any passing buses at least. We talked about this and that and completely failed to realise that the floor was moving until it was too late. With absolute horror, it dawned on us that we were walking through thousands of tiny frogs, and for the next few yards, we had to tip-toe so as not to commit some kind of froggy genocide.

To be honest, they could have been toads, as I do not really know the difference between the two, but when I mentioned this to my uncle later on, who is a bit of a wildlife fountain of knowledge, he told me that they probably were frogs based on my description. He then told me a few things about frogs, which are, quite frankly, quite weird creatures. For instance, I never knew that you could tell the sex of a frog by looking at its ears. Technically, a frog's ear is called a tympanum and is located just behind its eyes. If the tympanum is bigger than its eye, then it is male, and if it is smaller, it is female. Also, frogs drink not through their mouths but absorb moisture through their skin, which seems a bit pointless when they have such big mouths, and every time they hibernate, they grow a new layer of bone, which is how you tell the age of a frog. Of course, you would have to kill it, peel it, and saw through its bones, but there you go.

A furrowed field stood to our left, which according to the map, was the site of the deserted medieval village of Ravensthorpe. As deserted villages go, this one certainly lived up to its name, as there was literally nothing left.

Amazingly, there are thousands of deserted villages scattered all across the country, with the most important one being just a few miles away from this very spot, at a place called Wharram Percy. That one has been much studied, but more importantly, there are things to see, such as the ruined church, the village pond, as well as evidence of houses in the form of earthworks, and it is one of my favourite places to go. At Ravensthorpe, however, there was just a muddy field.

Skip back a thousand years, though, and this place would have been full of life, and it was even recorded in the Domesday Book, which is often misspelt as the Doomsday Book. And while many people have heard of the Domesday Book, not that many people actually know what it was or are aware that it is actually two books.

The book, or books, were commissioned by none other than William I, whom we also know, of course, as William the Conqueror. It was a survey of basically everything in the land, primarily so that he could get his filthy hands on it for him and his cronies. The name itself refers to the day of judgement and specifically to the fact that everything within the book is subject to the king's whim, and its decisions are therefore otherwise unalterable.

And we must remember that these two books, which are called Great Domesday and Little Domesday, are almost a thousand years old. That is maybe hard to appreciate, but I can say that some of my books are looking a bit raggedy after just a few years, so we can at least probably appreciate that it is amazing that they have survived at all.

But why are there two? Well, the first book - Great Domesday - contains the final summarized record of all the counties surveyed except Essex, Norfolk, and Suffolk, which were instead preserved in the second book - Little Domesday – and which were never summarized or added to the larger volume, and thus remained separate.

Not surprisingly, both books have been rebound several times over the years, not always for the better, but the latest attempt has probably restored the works as close to their original condition as they have been in a long while. Hopefully, they should last another thousand years, as they are currently kept in a controlled environment at 14 degrees Celsius and a relative humidity of 35%, which is apparently ideal for books but which would probably have me shivering, as I like it warm.

As for Ravensthorpe, it is not known when the village finally disappeared, although it was certainly long gone by the 1600s, nor is it known why it disappeared. Some suggest the plague or the black death, which occurred repeatedly and sporadically between the 1300s and the 1600s. It could have been farming changes, as, during the Middle Ages, wool became much more important. This meant less need for ridge and furrow farming and thus less need for labour, causing huge movements of people away from these villages. What is certain, though, is that for whatever reason, the people definitely left, which is exactly what we did next.

This section of the track had recently been somewhat pruned of trees, and countless logs lined the route of the path. This had me salivating, as I had recently had a wood burner installed in my house, and wood is very expensive. I did consider grabbing a rather large piece and popping it into Rob's rucksack, but as I couldn't even move it, I didn't bother.

As we walked, we heard sporadic gunfire coming from our left, although it was thankfully far away. We imagined it was coming from the nearby army base at Leconfield; either that or some local farmer had a rather large rabbit problem.

Leconfield had originally been an airbase and had housed the rather famous 616 Squadron, which had turned out to be the only squadron from Yorkshire that was ever involved in a major daytime air battle. It was originally an airfield designated for fighter aircraft, but as the tide of war turned gradually in favour of the allies, it was increasingly used as a bomber base and housed Polish and Free French crews, as well as British.

Later on, bombers from 640 Squadron, which was also based here, were involved in support bombing for D-Day, the allied invasion of France, bombing the area between Omaha and Utah beaches the night before troops landed on them. This was not without loss, however, and by the end of the war, this one squadron alone had lost 50 aircraft and 329 crew, a huge toll by any standard, even a wartime one.

The sound of traffic grew, and through the trees, we caught glimpses of passing cars and trucks, and in what seemed like no time at all, we were on the outskirts of Beverley.

A footbridge took us over the busy road and deposited us onto a sleepy housing estate, although there were worrying numbers of pensioners wandering around walking their labradoodles and old people dogs, most of which were sniffing us suspiciously, given our spicy state.

We made our way through a warren of streets, with windows twitching as we passed, and eventually, we found ourselves on a long and straight stretch of road leading directly towards the centre of the town.

Beverley is a nice place, and I imagine it would be very nice to live here, though perhaps just a little expensive, and it is said by those in the know that James Bond himself once nearly made this his permanent home. Daniel Craig was spotted house-hunting here just a few years ago, but he might just have been doing what we were doing, and going for a walk.

If I ever meet Mr Bond, I probably owe him an apology, as I was involved in a bit of an incident with him, or more accurately, with his car. I had been picking Sam up from the children's hospital in Leeds following his chemotherapy and was leaving the city during the rush hour, when I found my spritely little Ford Fiesta suddenly cut up by a rather fancy and expensive car with a private number plate. To say that I was not happy about this would be an understatement, as I just wanted to get him home.

I must confess that I was not a gentleman, and I did not let the car in, and it was only when it drove away that I managed to get a view of the driver, and when I also saw the private number plate which suggested a Bond theme, that I realised who it was. I did worry for a while about being whacked one night as I went out to empty the dustbin, but I guess he has forgiven me by now as I am quite clearly not dead yet, but on reflection, my conduct that day was somewhat below par. It's no excuse, but that's what stress does to you, I guess. Still, Mr Bond had the last laugh as he drove thirty yards up the road and entered the stream of traffic well ahead of me.

Whether or not it is true that Daniel Craig almost moved here, what is certain is that Beverley has rather a lot of history. St John of Beverley is from, well, Beverley, obviously, but another religious figure also has links to the town, and that would be Joan of Leeds.

Joan was a nun, from Leeds, of course, and hers is quite a funny story. She served at a convent called St Clementhorpe's, which, if you remember, we stopped near the site of while still in York. Basically, tired of the harsh life within the convent and the strict rules that this entailed, Joan did what any rational person would do. In 1318, she ran away and faked her own death and even went to the extremes of making a life-sized effigy of herself. Somewhat bizarrely, this effigy was then actually buried on holy ground purely and simply to convince the authorities that she really was dead. She then lived the rest of her life in a perpetual state of carnal lust and passion with some guy she had met along the way. Like I said, she did what any rational person would do under the circumstances. You couldn't make this stuff up.

This is not the first time this sort of tomfoolery had happened at St Clementhorpe, either. Quite extraordinarily, nun running was actually a somewhat common occurrence there, and the local archbishop even had to take steps to stop this sort of thing from happening, presumably because, at some point, they found themselves running out of nuns.

For instance, just a few years before Joan ran off, a similar case occurred in 1301, which was just as funny, if not more so. Another nun, this one going by the name of Cecily, was out walking one day when she met a group of men on horseback by the priory gate. Witnesses said that she threw off her habit, put on some normal clothes, and jumped on a horse with one of the men. She then disappeared forever, at least as far as the convent was concerned, and it is said that she lived the rest of her life with a bloke called Gregg up in the frozen north that is otherwise known as Darlington.

It happened again, too, in 1310, coincidentally to another nun called Joan, though it was definitely a different Joan, as I checked. Although the records don't indicate exactly what it was that this Joan is said to have done, she was later forbidden from receiving visitors, was told that she had to be accompanied by other nuns at all times, and was expressly forbidden from fraternising with someone called Lady Alice de Walleys, who had been accused of *lapses of the flesh,* whatever that meant.

These lapses of the flesh were never defined, so we will have to use our imaginations, I suggested to Rob. He gave me a rather strange look, and I immediately realised what I had said and how weird it had sounded, but it was too late.

Anyway, yet another nun, this one called Isabella, had also been accused of *lapses of the flesh*, which suggests that St Clementhorpe was perhaps more of a brothel than a convent, but there you go. And this behaviour wasn't just down to the ladies either. In 1313, the archbishop had to deal with Brother John, who was accused of sexual intimacy with a nun known as Alice of Leeds. As the story goes, this was spiritual incest because, in the eyes of the church, John and Alice were brother and sister in the service of God. It certainly sounds like all concerned had a really good time at the convent, and not surprisingly, it is no longer there, but how could it be, as everyone ran away.

Beverley has a few more people to shout about, too. Ken Annakin was also born here, and if you haven't heard of him, you might have seen one of his films. He directed such classic movies as *The Battle of the Bulge* and *The Call of the Wild* and was a big name back in his day. For years, there were rumours that George Lucas took Annakin's name for the character of Anakin Skywalker in the Star Wars franchise, but following Annakin's death in 2009, and I mean Ken Annakin, not Anakin Skywalker, Lucas finally confirmed that this was one rumour that was not actually true, which is a shame. It would, after all, be great to be able to claim that Anakin Skywalker was from Yorkshire.

Artist Frederick Elwell also hailed from Beverley and was a prolific painter who left behind more than 500 works of art following his death. To say he was a good painter would be an understatement, and he was even commissioned to paint a portrait of the king in 1932, King George V, by his wife, Queen Mary. The painting is very nice, although, for some reason, the queen was not happy with it and requested several alterations.

Thomas Percy is yet another famous son of Beverley, but they don't really shout about this one. He was, at least for a long time, something of an embarrassment to the town, as he was, in fact, one of the main conspirators of the Gunpowder Plot that aimed to blow King James and Parliament sky high in 1605 and is thus another one of the reasons that I do stupid things with fireworks at least once a year.

In the run-up to the plot, Percy spent much of his time in London, along with someone who was supposed to be his servant, a man going by the name of John Johnson. Johnson's real name was someone you might have heard of, as he was, in fact, a certain Guy Fawkes, who we met back at York. And John Johnson, let's face it, was not a very original alias, which tells us that Fawkes probably thought of this name in something of a hurry, or more accurately, he didn't think at all.

When the plot was ultimately discovered, and when Fawkes was caught red-handed directly underneath Parliament, complete with 36 barrels of gunpowder and enough fuses to blow the whole thing to smithereens, he initially used his own false name but inexplicably gave his master's real name of Thomas Percy, which was not very nice when you think about it. Percy went on the run straight away, disappearing off to the north of England, so the government brought in an astrologer to gaze into a crystal ball to locate him.

And they did find him, too, at Holbeche House in Staffordshire, although not because of the astrologer. On the way up to Holbeche House, Percy and Catesby and the other plotters had taken gunpowder and supplies from Warwick Castle, which obviously attracted rather a lot of attention. However, the weather then turned incredibly bad, and the gunpowder became rather damp during the rest of the journey.

When they arrived at Holbeche, then, someone had the bright idea of putting the gunpowder in front of the fire to dry out. It doesn't take a bright spark, if you pardon the pun, to imagine what happened next, and to cut a long story short, the pile of gunpowder ignited and blew the whole place up, severely damaging the house and injuring several of the plotters. It also called even more attention to Catesby and Percy and the rest of them, and when the king's men finally turned up, there was a rather short siege followed by an even shorter battle.

Percy was shot along with Catesby, and legend

has it they even died by the same musket ball. They were both buried within the grounds of the house, but a short while later, their bodies were exhumed on the orders of the king, and their heads were lopped off and taken to London to be put on spikes outside Parliament, and that was the end of that.

We wandered through Beverley and soon found ourselves passing the police station, which reminded me that famous outlaw Dick Turpin was held in Beverley before being shipped off to York for his trial and ultimate execution and who we had popped to see at the beginning of our journey, of course.

Turpin had been living under his fake name of John Palmer in Brough, a few miles to our south, but had been arrested after getting into an argument and shooting someone's chicken, which seems a somewhat trivial way to catch one of the most wanted men in England at that time.

Palmer was brought here then, to Beverley, where the authorities took a bit of a closer look at him and realised all was not as it seemed. Charges of horse theft were brought against him, a very serious charge indeed that carried the death penalty for those convicted, which explains why he was sent to York, as that was where the main court was. Once in York, his true identity was finally discovered, and the rest, as they say, is history.

We carried on, passing beneath the beautiful castle-like North Bar, a curious construction that once acted as the medieval entrance to the town and also as a toll booth. Indeed, ancient records show that this was, in fact, the main entrance to the town, judging by the number of tolls collected.

While the gap beneath the bar may have been big enough for horses and carts, the advent of the twentieth century and the introduction of double-decker buses posed new problems, and after one or two incidents, the local bus company introduced specially shaped buses that they said could better navigate the bar without the risk of smashing it to bits. The photos, however, tell a different story and suggest mere inches of clearance above the roof, and I, for one, would not like to drive a bus through it, regardless of the shape of the roof.

We were heading for a small church, St Mary's, but first, I wanted to stop at the shop that stood on the corner of North Bar Within and Waltham Lane. Had the Germans actually invaded England during the war, you see, then this very shop would probably have been one of the most important places in the country. This is because the special auxiliary units that we last heard of back at Kilnwick Percy have a very strong but somewhat secret link to this very building.

At the time, the building was a humble sweet shop, not that there were many sweets to be had in the war, which is kind of a clue if you ask me, as it was hardly ever open. Anyway, the original door that led from the front of the shop into the rear was sealed up, and a new side door was knocked straight through the gable end wall on Waltham Lane. Following a German landing, then, this building would have been the headquarters of every secret auxiliary unit from as far north as Northumberland and as far south as the River Thames.

Curiously, as we passed, the door was open, and shop-fitters were busy inside ripping the place apart. I spoke to one of them, Keith, and asked him if they had come across anything odd about the shop, and I also explained a bit of its history to him.

He seemed interested and took us inside for a look, and he suggested that the layout today was certainly not the original one. He had worked in other stores on this row, he went on, and this one had definitely been altered. I was hoping he would tell us that they had found hand grenades and secret codes hidden in the walls, but all they had found, he said, were cobwebs.

We thanked him for letting us in and wandered off down the road for a quick look at the Beverley Arms Hotel. It was here that William Wilberforce spent the famous 1807 election that saw him win a great victory and which had, in fact, been the first election held in Yorkshire since 1742, a staggering sixty-five-year gap. Although there were elections called between these two dates, the landed aristocracy had always put it upon themselves to decide on the candidates to be put forward for appointment, thereby negating the need for the lower classes to decide who to vote for, just in case we got it wrong.

The voting wasn't held here, though, and the hotel was what we would nowadays call his campaign headquarters. Wilberforce and his staff instead arranged carriages to take voters from here all the way back to York, where we started, of course, where their vote would be registered in the castle yard. Apparently, this strange arrangement caused tremendous traffic jams throughout Yorkshire for the fifteen days that it took to register all of the votes, and every night the newspapers would publish *the state of the poll,* as voting was a matter for the public record back then, which at least made it easy to see which way the election was going. Wilberforce took the lead on the fourth day, a lead which he never lost, and was returned as the Member of Parliament for the area, beating his rival Henry Lascelles by a wide margin, despite Lascelles having spent far more money campaigning than Wilberforce had.

We didn't go in, as it looked rather swanky, and we were, well, let's just say we were not. Instead, we wandered to the church across the road, which was St Mary's, and which I told Rob we simply had to pop into. We had a look at the outside first, and I told Rob to look up, as there were some rather interesting carvings to be seen. We had soon spotted one, then two, then three, and altogether we counted at least a dozen, and they were all new, I told Rob.

When the church was built around eight hundred years ago, the builders placed lots of sculptures way up high. Over the years, however, these have slowly eroded away to the point that it was impossible to see what they had originally been, so over the last few years, a scheme has been run to install new ones.

The carvings we could see high above us today were all of historically important women and feature the likes of Marie Curie, famous for advances in the treatment of cancer, Amy Johnson, a famous aviator from nearby Hull, as well as more modern examples such as Helen Sharman who was the first British person to go into space and who is also from Yorkshire. However, the one we were looking for today was none other than Hilda Lyon, inventor of the Lyon shape that made submarines so cool and whom we had come across in Market Weighton, and we finally found her after much deliberation. It was definitely her, we decided, as she was clutching something that clearly resembled an airship.

There is another treat to be found on the church, too, and it is even better, I promised Rob. Also up there are carvings of an altogether different, and might I say much more fun nature. Far above your heads, if you take the time to look, you will also find some fantastic carvings of characters from *The Lion, the Witch and the Wardrobe,* the curiously named fantastical tale written by the even more curiously named Clive Staples Lewis, a name which probably explains why everyone calls him CS Lewis. These were much easier to see, and in no time at all, we had managed to find Aslan the lion, Farsight the eagle, as well as the White Witch, of course.

There are fourteen of them altogether, and while the lion Aslan is perhaps the most recognisable, my favourite was definitely Mr Tumnus, the faun, who is half man and half goat. I particularly liked him because he looked just a little bit crazy and reminded me of my good friend Chris, who is also just a little bit crazy. Furthermore, CS Lewis wrote that the idea for the story came to him from a single picture he had in his head of a faun carrying an umbrella, so there you go.

Going from one Lewis to another, there is a second literary connection within this church, this one regarding not CS Lewis but Lewis

Carroll, whose real name was actually Charles Lutwidge Dodgson, by the way. On an archway within the building is a rather fun carving of a rabbit, who is not only stood up like a human but appears to be wearing a jacket and sporting a pocket watch, too. Furthermore, the rabbit appears to be holding some kind of bag and bears a rather striking resemblance to the white rabbit from Alice in Wonderland, and it is this carving that is said by some to have given Carroll the original idea for his rabbit.

We popped inside the church as well, as there was something else I wanted to look for but which I had not managed to find as yet. While Beverley was largely spared damage from bombing during the Second World War, there were one or two incidents. The most serious was a 500-kilogram bomb that was dropped on Flemingate at 5.55pm on the August Bank Holiday in 1942, which killed a couple of people and damaged quite a few houses. At the time, Flemingate was the main road through the town, and despite the damage, the civil defence crews had the fires out and the road open by 10pm the same night. This is pretty much amazing when you consider that it takes the average council around six months to repair a single pothole, but there you go. Anyway, it was said at the time that the death toll was so low because it was a bank holiday and many people had gone to the seaside, and dozens more had gone to the local cinema to watch Old Mother Riley, who was ultimately given huge credit as a life-saver in the town.

The second concerned this church. Relatively early on in the war, on October 17th, 1940, a lone German bomber had flown over the town and machine-gunned many of the streets. Nobody was killed, but two men were shot in the feet, which sounds funny but must have surely hurt, and several buildings were damaged, including this church. In fact, a bullet was found lodged in a pew, and it was the bullet hole I was looking for, but it was a long time ago, so I suspected the pew in question was no longer here.

I could not have been more wrong, though. I went over to have a chat with one of the church wardens, who immediately escorted me directly to the pew with the bullet hole, and it was still in the same place where it had been when it was shot. Furthermore, she showed me the pew behind and pointed out the spot where the bullet had finally lodged itself, though she added that some cheeky children had turned up pretty quickly and promptly stolen it. She was clearly of the intellectual type and was highly intelligent, so my attempt to add to the conversation with my observation that the sound a bullet makes as it flies past you is also pew did not go down very well. Anyhow, she went on to show me the exact spot where the bullet flew through the window, where you could see that the repair work to the glass was slightly different to the original which surrounded it, and she then pointed out the alignment between the two holes in the pews and the hole in the window, which formed a satisfyingly straight line, much as you would expect.

Beverley, as I said, was largely lucky in not getting bombed directly, but the people of the town were certainly still hugely affected by the war. They really got stuck right in, as well, with the first-ever demonstration of air raid precautions being given in Beverley in February of 1939.

In October of the next year, an old American battleship was renamed HMS Beverley, and the people of the town generously sent volumes of gifts to the crew. Many residents opened their homes to children evacuated from Hull, just a few miles to the south, which was thought by many to be a huge target largely due to the docks. They were proven right, too. On the night of May 7th, 1941, many people from Beverley were forced to watch in horror as Hull burned after being badly blitzed by one of the largest raids of the war so far, a fact which was kept highly secret, with Hull being referred to simply as a *north east coast town*.

Christmas of 1942 was perhaps a low point for Beverley. The country's infrastructure had been severely pummelled, and low water levels meant that water supplies were cut off every night. The bad luck continued into 1943, and on the 8th of May, the people of the town read the sad news that HMS Beverley had been lost in action. They would have had no idea, of course, that exactly two years after that very date, they would emerge victorious with the end of the war in Europe, so it must have been a very grim time indeed.

In August 1943, intrigue visited the town in a rather strange manner. The local rag and bone man mysteriously vanished and was replaced by someone with a huge, bushy, ginger beard. Somewhat curiously, the imposter was then arrested as a German spy, causing much excitement for the local gossip brigade. All in all, Beverley had about as interesting a war as anyone would really want to and was ultimately very lucky to come out largely unscathed, particularly the minster. It is thought that, like other historic landmarks, these buildings were left untouched as they acted as excellent navigation points for German pilots, which makes perfect sense.

They were acting as navigation points for us today as well. All the while, as we wandered through Beverley, we had been continuously teased by short and intermittent sightings of the huge towers of Beverley Minster, the huge cathedral-like church that dominated the town as well as the surrounding countryside.

We finally found ourselves at the foot of it and gaped up in awe at the huge towers shooting straight up before us, something which brought on a certain feeling of dizziness for me.

The minster owes its existence to St John, of course, and he is still buried within the building in a vault somewhere beneath the nave, which is perhaps not surprising. He might have been inadvertently cremated at some point, though, as a huge fire destroyed not only the minster but most of the town way back in 1188. During the rebuild, Henry III provided forty oak trees from Sherwood Forest, which was surely very nice of him, but the work progressed incredibly slowly, and the two huge towers did not go up until around the year 1400. Curiously, it is these two towers that later gave Nicholas Hawksmoor the inspiration for the towers of Westminster Abbey, the copycat, though they did not go up until the early 1800s, which somewhat surprised me, as I had always presumed them to be much older.

Anyway, by the early 1700s, Beverley Minster was subsiding, and some of it was in danger of collapse. Several buttresses had to be built to shore up the walls, some of which were by now overhanging the base by up to four feet. Much of this work was supervised by Nicholas Hawksmoor, which is presumably when he got the idea for his towers at Westminster Abbey, though they were not actually built until after his death.

And if the minster looks familiar, then it is possibly because it is a film star. It has appeared regularly in the historical drama *Victoria* which helped Jenna Coleman become rather rich and famous, and it has also featured in, among other things, a drama called *Gunpowder*, which tells the story of Robert Catesby and Thomas Percy and their buddies who tried to blow parliament up, which is rather fitting considering the town's links to the plot.

Also, one of the stars of the show, Kit Harrington, who voiced a character in one of my son's favourite cartoon movies, *How to Train Your Dragon,* but is perhaps even better known for playing the character of Jon Snow in *Game of Thrones*, is actually directly related to Robert Catesby, who if you remember is one of the conspirators of the gunpowder plot. This is kind of cool and just goes to show that the universe really does have a plan or at least a sense of humour. To further illustrate this point, Harrington's full name is actually Christopher Catesby Harrington. You couldn't make it up.

The minster seemed like a good place to stop, and we found a bench outside near some kind of engraved stone or rock, which bizarrely had something resembling a swastika scratched out on it, which quite frankly left us a bit discombobulated. We sat there and discussed it while we waited for our lift, which today was my wife, and we ultimately decided that it was back to front, and therefore not an actual swastika in the nasty horrible fascist sense, so all was once again well with the universe.

In fact, the swastika was, for thousands of years, a symbol of good fortune and was merely hijacked by the Nazis in the 1930s, which has left it tainted forevermore. And there are swastikas all over England, not just here in Beverley. There is a rather famous one on Ilkley Moor, set high above the town, and there is even one on a government building in London, quite surprisingly on the Foreign and Commonwealth Office. Even Rudyard Kipling was a fan of the symbol, and if you are lucky enough to own an early copy of The Jungle Book, check the spine, and you will probably be surprised to find a bloody big swastika on it.

I realised that I had not phoned my wife to give her a time to pick us up, so I quickly did so. Rob looked puzzled as I dialled her number and let it ring a few times, and then disconnected the call. He stayed silent but was clearly perplexed, and after a long and uncomfortable silence, he finally asked me what I was doing. I explained that I would ring her back in a few seconds, but this was clearly not a satisfactory explanation for my follically challenged friend. The first call is just a heads-up, I went on, and gives her the chance to rake through her handbag, pulling out all the useless crap such as the first aid kit we've had since the kids were little, that membership card for the gym she's never been to, as well as her broomstick. The second call is the actual call, I told him, and by the time I ring back, she has usually found her phone and cleaned it of jelly babies and the like.

Feeling smug, I promptly re-dialled, which left me completely let down, as she still didn't answer, so instead, I sent her a text.

We were very much enjoying this walk, and all was well apart from the fact that we only had one last stretch of it to go. That stretch would take us firmly and finally home, and all the way back to Hull, an often-underestimated little city that actually has a richer and deeper history than you could possibly imagine, but please don't tell anybody, as I don't want it overrun by groups of interestingly clad tourists.

I didn't know it at the time, but we actually had one final surprise for the day. When my wife picked me up, she had brought my mother-in-law along. How thoughtful of her, I remarked.

Don't get me wrong. I love my mother-in-law, although she can be a bit scary, but then I guess she's only doing her job. I recently discovered that she has weekly sessions with Lucifer himself on how to be even more evil. I've no idea what kind of fees she's charging him, though.

Anyway, I have promised my wife that if anything ever happens to her, I will take great care of her mother. For instance, one day, I will take her to one of those spas where the little fishes eat your dead skin for just a small fee. It will be way cheaper than putting her in the cemetery.

When I die, though, I think I'm going to get cremated, if only for the reason that it will be my one and only chance to have a smokin' hot body. I hope I don't die yet, though, as I am rather enjoying this little walk of ours, and I would rather like to finish it, as the next stage looks really good.

A Wonky End
Beverley to Hull (Amost)

Rob's wife dropped us off outside of the minster, almost at the exact point that we finished last time. This was very kind of her, and she even almost stopped the car for us, and was only going around five or ten miles per hour when she told us to get out as she was in a hurry to get to work.

I mentioned to Rob that she's getting more and more considerate of us as we slowly morph into old men, but he said that the morphing wasn't all that slow anymore, and I think he was right.

We wandered over to the swastika stone so we could be confident that we really had started off from where we had finished, and I rubbed that not-a-swastika for good luck, an act which I think alarmed Rob.

Today, the plan was to follow the route out

of Beverley and take a leisurely amble along the River Hull, heading south towards the town of the same name. Technically it's a city, but Hull has the feel of a town as far as I am concerned, so that is what I would be calling it today, and I might even bounce between the two randomly just to liven things up a little.

Before we moved on, though, we decided to have a wander around the massive minster, which was great, as it's free to get in.

Someone at the door greeted us with a wary look, presumably because they had seen the huge backpacks that we were kitted out with today. We had, you see, decided to carry a full load just to remind us what it would be like to try to cripple yourself with dozens of kilograms of your finest junk, as that was exactly what we would be doing in a few weeks when hopefully we would be doing a longer walk.

We had cunningly persuaded our better halves to let us sneak off for a walk along Offa's Dyke you see, which runs along the English and Welsh border, and we would be carrying everything with us and camping along the way, what with the route being so far from our homes.

My bag weighed in at around twenty kilograms, while Rob's must have been around twenty-five, and both were pretty huge. The warden was clearly alarmed at us coming into the church and possibly destroying some priceless artifact when we inevitably swung around, so he suggested we leave them with him.

Rob was fine with this, but I was suspicious and suspected he was some kind of deviant, but we left them anyway and went for a look around.

The minster was more or less deserted, and there were probably less than a dozen people inside it altogether. We did a full circuit, and I found a map of the place on the wall, which I took a photo of so we wouldn't get lost.

We started at the north transept, where the map promised us a leaning pillar. While it was no Leaning Tower of Pisa, it was impressively wonky and almost seemed to be defying gravity.

We moved on to a display that told of ancient Beverley being a place of sanctuary, something that attracted all sorts of criminals to the area in the past and which is probably one of the things that drew in Rob's ancestors, I suggested. In fact, there are three sanctuary stones around Beverley that define the borders of where you could and couldn't claim sanctuary, and within this minster, there is something called the *fridstool*, which means *the chair of peace*, which is basically a sanctuary chair. This is a very rare chair indeed, and the only other known example is at Hexham Abbey up in Northumberland, co-incidentally where St. John of Beverley was the bishop. In other places, a stone chair was usually used in the oath-making that accompanied the process of giving a fugitive the right of sanctuary, and although no direct evidence of this exists in Beverley, it is fair to assume that the same happened here.

We next passed the final resting place of St John of Beverley and then crossed the nave to admire the statues of St John as well as one of King Athelstan, who is said to have been the one that granted the town its sanctuary status in the first place, or more accurately, he formalised it and made it official.

We then wandered back across the nave to admire something called the *wrongly placed pillar*, which was clearly marked on the map, but as I had a good look over it, I could not figure out what it was exactly that made it wrongly placed.

Luckily, the weirdo that had been so interested in our bags was now here, after presumably selling all of our stuff on the internet, so I went to ask him what it was that made this pillar so wrong.

He was actually very nice, and I immediately decided that he wasn't any kind of deviant after all but was just a bit of a geek. He knew his stuff, too, and had soon pointed out that all of the pillars in this row were out of line with all of the pillars in the other row, which was obvious once you knew and had taken a look.

He went on to tell us that this made one of the towers a couple of feet smaller than the rest, which was entirely due to the pillars being out of alignment. If the towers had been built the same size, he told us, you would have a wonky end, and nobody likes a wonky end, he stated, and I guess he was right. I really liked this guy, I decided.

Having spent far too long in here, we decided to grab our bags and make a move. Immediately blinded by the brilliant sunshine outside, we decided to do a lap of the church before moving on, which proved really worthwhile when Rob stood in some dog poo, and I tripped on a kerb.

The minster didn't seem as big on the outside, and it only took us a couple of minutes to walk around it, so we were soon heading up Friars Lane, which led us, funnily enough, to Beverley Friary. This beautiful old building was once home to Dominican monks, who were a part of the Catholic Church, but it now hosts smelly hikers and backpackers like us, having been a youth hostel since the early 1980s. It is mere luck that the friary is still here at all, though. The place was originally much larger, but King Henry VIII demolished much of it in the 1500s, and the 1800s saw yet more of it knocked down to build the railway line that runs right past it today. In the 1960s, someone else had the bright idea of smashing the rest of it into rubble and building a housing estate, but luckily the council immediately slapped a preservation order on what was left of it, which finally put an end to all such lunacy.

It's a good job they did, too, because, during a recent renovation, builders found some of the most impressive medieval wall paintings ever to have been discovered anywhere. Although we didn't go in today as there didn't seem to be anybody around, I had seen the paintings a few years ago, and they are basically the medieval equivalent of wallpaper and were apparently quite common until someone invented actual wallpaper. I remember that my favourite one had depicted blackbirds, and the guide had told me that they were supposed to be a comical representation of the friars themselves, who wore black cloaks, and who were therefore probably somewhat scary if you bumped into one late at night.

There were none around today, though, so we plodded on, crossing a footbridge over the railway line and heading towards a rather fancy new shopping centre.

The place was heaving, and countless people were enjoying drinks al fresco, and we briefly considered joining them but figured if we did so, that would be the end of our walk. We couldn't really stop anyway, as we had only walked a few hundred yards, so we would have to wait a while longer, though we did stop and support the local economy with our purchase of two rather nice sausage sandwiches and a couple of large coffees.

We sat briefly on a bench while we stuffed ourselves silly, resting our backpacks and therefore our backs at the same time, but did not actually take them off again as we couldn't be bothered. Countless shoppers passed us by, with one or two of them giving us funny looks, so I guess we were sort of out of place.

We'd normally find ourselves wandering through forests and fields, and although we had occasionally skirted various towns and cities on our many walks, we had never done this so near to our homes, and it just felt odd. And then it dawned on me that at some point, we were probably going to bump into somebody we knew, and they might well wonder why we were traipsing around our own backyard wearing giant rucksacks. We could just tell them we were shoplifters, I said to Rob. Really good ones.

We vacated our bench and moved on when an elderly couple came along. It's not that they smelt or anything; it was just that they looked a bit rickety on their feet, and we figured they needed a sit down more than us.

The shops petered out, and we wandered through a small housing estate before joining the main road out of the town, where a statue briefly distracted us as we passed the canal head. We wandered over to it to see who it was and discovered it was not one particular person but was a depiction of a creeler. I had no idea what a creeler was, but the statue featured a rather miserable looking bloke holding a sack, and when we read the small plaque, we realised why he looked so miserable. A creeler, it turned out, was basically a labourer who unloaded barges at this spot and then carried the cargo all the way to the town centre.

Apparently, this quiet spot, where the canal stops at what is now a very pretty and tranquil place, was once one of the busiest places imaginable. Around a thousand years ago, believe it or not, Beverley was a major inland port and one of the biggest towns in the country. Mills lined the canal as well, adding industry to the busy goings-on of the port, with the chief exports being wool and something called whitening. Made from chalk, whitening was exactly what you might expect it to be, and was used in building material, paints, flour and chocolate, and this area was one of the major sources of the stuff. And an informative sign told us all sorts of stuff about the town, such as why Flemingate was called thus called. Years ago, Flemish cloth merchants made their home there, and the name has clearly stuck.

As we moved on once again, Rob suggested

that we call ourselves creelers for the rest of the day, as we basically had large and heavy sacks on our backs, so with our most miserable faces on, we carried on our merry way.

We crossed a busy road near a small shopping park right at the edge of town and briefly found ourselves on a small section of the old road, seemingly abandoned when the roundabout had been built. Nature was slowly taking over, with small weeds beginning to appear through the cracks in the tarmac, and the kerbstones were slowly beginning to disintegrate.

This led us into an interesting chat about how long it would take nature to totally remove all signs of humans in the event that everyone suddenly disappeared. Rob reckoned that it would take thousands of years, but I reckoned most things would be gone much quicker than that. I thought this for one reason, I told him, which was a small weed that I had seen popping through some tarmac a while back. The thing that struck me was that the tarmac, which had been laid on a small path just near my house, had only been down for a couple of weeks when I first saw that tiny little weed poking through it, and it is something that has stuck with me ever since.

Buildings and structures would collapse, weakened by tree roots. Wind and rain would erode all manner of materials, and I reckoned that within a few hundred years, nature would have completely retaken more or less everything that was around us now, at least on the visible level.

Rob scoffed at this and suggested that it would take a very long time indeed for nature to take back large buildings and bridges and other large structures. I asked him if he included himself in that, but I don't think he heard me.

Because we were deep in intellectual conversation, basically talking a load of old tosh, we missed the gate that should have taken us across some fields and towards the River Hull. We realised our mistake when we arrived at what looked to be some kind of industrial estate and briefly considered turning back, but then Rob had a better idea. We could simply hop the fence, he said, and by the time I had processed what he had said, he'd already done it.

It was perhaps easier for him to do this, given his lofty legs, but for me, it was more of a challenge, especially considering that I had a rather large backpack on. It was perhaps exactly this that unbalanced me, and I had visions of falling to my death directly into a large cowpat that had been sitting and waiting patiently for at least a week for some poor schmuck like me to come along.

Luckily, I managed to grab hold of the fence, so I did not encounter a fate worse than death, much to Rob's disappointment. I think he was also getting his camera ready to gather some evidence of my ineptitude, and he looked very disappointed when he had to tuck it back into his pocket, unused.

We made our way across the field, dodging yet more cowpats, which was odd, as there were no cows around. Sheep and horses, yes, but cows, no.

We found what appeared to be a track, and upon joining it, we reckoned we were back on the actual path we had intended to follow, and it led us through what was a very pleasant meadow. All of this area is common land, and by all accounts, Beverley has some of the best common land in the country. If you happen to live here, then you might well find you have the right to come and graze your cattle here, if you have any, that is. Quite bizarrely, up until 1978, nobody actually knew who owned the land as such, which is when a court decided that it actually belonged to the local council. They weren't very happy about this, of course, as ever since then, they have had to pay considerable sums of money for the upkeep of it all. Still, they are doing a fine job, as it is now a green oasis of tranquillity and a great place to take your cow for a walk.

This thought reminded me of a funny story I had read about a cow, which I now shared with

Rob. It related to a vet in the Netherlands who had been fined by the local courts for burning down a farm. He hadn't done it deliberately but had merely been trying to demonstrate to a farmer that his cows were passing too much gas. He did this by using a lighter to set fire to one of the cow's farts, which is something you would expect a drunken teenager to do, quite frankly, and not a highly qualified professional, but then blokes are just blokes, no matter how many letters we have after our names. Anyway, quite unexpectedly, for the vet at least, the cow basically turned into a four-legged flamethrower and ran around in something of a panic, setting several hay bales alight as it did so. The resulting inferno spread to the rest of the farm and caused tens of thousands of pounds worth of damage, though somehow, the cow remained unharmed, although it was presumably quite pissed off.

We soon found ourselves skirting what looked like a primordial swamp, with flooded areas enveloping several large trees, before joining a path that led us along the edge of what we thought was the river, but which turned out to be one of the many ditches that have been built around here over the centuries to drain the land.

This one was wide and impressive, and had the look of a canal more than a ditch, and was clearly a haven for wildlife. Birds tweeted in the trees, and rabbits darted away from us as we made our way along, and up above us, some kind of bird of prey hovered steadily, presumably while looking for a spot of lunch. As we approached, it made an extremely rapid and rather impressive freefall dive towards the earth, disappearing behind some trees. This was when I told Rob that he should have put a hat on, as the sun had probably been glinting off his shiny bald head and had perhaps blinded the poor feathery thing.

A fence told us that we were leaving the pastures, or more accurately, if we had been travelling in the opposite direction, it would welcome us into them. It wasn't much of a welcome, though, and I suggested to Rob that the pasture masters were, how can I put this, miserable old farts. The sign, you see, after specifically welcoming you onto the land, totally prohibited you from actually doing anything on it, just in case you got any funny ideas.

Want to come here for a barbecue? No chance. Don't even think about it. Don't think about camping here, either, and certainly don't bring your car. Don't bring your bike, for that matter, as cycling is prohibited here too. And if you think that this nice open space would be a good and safe place to let Spot or Fido or Steve or whatever your precious little pooch is called have a little run, well, you'd better think again. Oh, and if you do bring your beloved canine, the sign asked you to please pick up after it, and although this seems like a reasonable request, I should perhaps just remind you that the whole place is knee-deep in cow shit, thank you very much.

Rob was slowly edging away from me as I had my little rant, much like you might do when you encounter a random lunatic or perhaps even a drunken person while out and about, and when I finally caught up with him, we noticed that the landscape had changed completely.

We were now wandering through farmers' fields, all freshly planted with whatever delights would pop up in three months or so, and after a few minutes, we came across what appeared to be the farmhouse.

It was certainly different, and I commented to Rob that I had never seen a Yorkshire farmhouse built in the style of a Mexican hacienda, with rendered walls and terracotta tiles reminding me of many wild west movies from my youth. Rob concurred and added that he had equally never seen such a fine ass either, which gave me pause for thought. He went on, however, to point out what appeared to be a carved wooden donkey above and behind a hedge, so technically, what he said was pretty accurate, as it really was a very nice ass indeed.

We came to a road and became somewhat confused, which is never difficult, not for two elderly and somewhat thick wanderers such as ourselves. The map suggested that the footpath carried on straight ahead and that we should continue following the drain, but a fence barred our way. We would normally just hop over it, but it was decorated with some rather nice barbed wire, and past incidents have taught us not to be so bloody stupid. The bulls in the field on the other side of the fence didn't look too friendly, either, and they looked like they could probably run pretty fast when they needed to, such as when they were chasing two chubby old hikers.

There was no obvious sign pointing the way, so we wandered across the bridge and examined the next field, where we decided that we could sort of see where people had walked and that we would follow in their footsteps.

Nobody shouted at us or set their dogs on us, so we must have made the right decision, and we were soon walking straight into the sun, heading more or less due south.

We crossed another road, where we found a fingerpost that confirmed we were on the right track after all, but as we stepped up onto the road from behind a rather portly bush, a white van raced past, almost squashing Rob's toes.

The next section saw us passing some rather plush houses which backed right onto the drain. One enterprising individual had even built a gate and some decking, upon which they had placed a couple of chairs and a small table. Although it was only a drain and not a canal or river as such, it was probably still very nice to sit down there on a nice sunny evening sipping a gin and tonic or whatever floats your boat, though I imagine you might get somewhat bitten by things with small wings and very sharp teeth.

The main road was next, which was odd, as we had become accustomed to almost total isolation since leaving Beverley, and we now found ourselves attempting to cross one of the busiest roads around here, apparently at the busiest time of day.

We could only see a few yards in either direction, as our crossing was unfortunately positioned between two bends in the road, one on either side of us. Of course, as soon as we stepped out into what we thought was a gap in the traffic, vehicles simultaneously appeared from both directions, intent on mowing us down.

I'm not saying I got a close look at the driver of the ridiculously tiny red car that tried to murder me, but he had a rather scary mole on the end of his nose, which was presumably the reason why he couldn't see where he was driving.

We checked to see if we could continue along the bank of this beautiful waterway, but alas, we could not. A brick wall blocked our way on one side, and fences looked like they would stop us from getting far on the other, so we did as the map suggested and followed the road for a bit.

Dunswell was ahead of us, which is a little nothing of a village, though strangely, it does have two pubs. I had read that people used to call it *Beerhouses* exactly for this reason, which is a much better name than Dunswell, it has to be said. Perhaps ironically, the hall in the village is called Sober Hall, which we passed and which looked very nice indeed, though it was perhaps a little boring.

Traffic passed us by along with the odd jogger and cyclist, but we didn't have to put up with the deprivations of society for very long. After a few hundred yards, we turned down a small lane almost opposite a pub called The Ship Inn, and we were once again more or less immediately enjoying suburban tranquillity.

I say more or less immediately because there was a slight disturbance that greeted us as we turned onto this leafy lane. One of the residents looked to be operating a small car repair business and actually had lots of nice classic Land Rovers parked on his drive.

He was an elderly gentleman, and we exchanged pleasantries as we passed him and whoever he was talking to, who was another even older man. They were discussing the car that was badly parked on the road there, and at first, I thought they were chuntering or complaining about it until the older of the two climbed in and started the engine.

This surprised me, as the car in question was a battered old Honda which had been modified with blacked-out windows, lowered suspension, a bright red paint job, and, according to the sound which immediately emanated from the back of it, the engine from a Typhoon fighter jet.

Rob looked at me with raised eyebrows, as he was equally surprised at this turn of events, and after having a quick glance over our shoulders to double-check what we had seen, we wandered away through an increasingly thick cloud of burning rubber and exhaust fumes as a random grandad pulled doughnuts somewhere behind us. Interestingly and perhaps coincidentally, doughnut is defined in the Oxford English dictionary as someone who is extremely stupid and who lacks intelligence and common sense. I am not implying anything. I am just saying.

Further up the road, we met a crazy lady who was stuffing things into her car and babbling away to herself. As we approached, her head popped out, and she gave us a quick hello, and she looked a bit embarrassed. She explained that she wasn't actually talking to herself but was putting her baby into the car, so we gave her a nice smile and said hello.

I looked into the car as we passed and managed to catch an unfortunate glimpse of possibly the ugliest baby on the planet. It had a hairy scrunched-up face and goofy teeth, and it also appeared to be cross-eyed and rather stupid looking.

It was then that I realised that it was a dog and was not, in fact, an actual baby as such, and I think Rob realised this at the same time as I did, judging by his huge sigh of relief. Specifically, it was a pug, and it was actually a rather cute one. I did consider stealing it for a second or two and shoving it in my backpack, and taking it home. Its head would look really cute sticking out of the top of my bag, I thought, but because I didn't want the extra weight, or the complication of police people chasing me across the countryside with helicopters and tasers and the like, we plodded on.

We soon joined the riverbank, which meant we would now spend the next few miles walking along the banks of the mighty River Hull, which would, of course, take us home. The river here meanders gently through the flat countryside, snaking its way through what was previously farmland but which was now slowly morphing into a housing estate.

We must have been near the official boundary,

and it seems like the authorities intend to get their money's worth and have built right up to the city limits. The houses all look more or less the same, and while I am sure they are very nice, in the back of my mind, I found myself wondering what would happen the next time the river flooded.

This happened a few years back, and large parts of the city became temporary fish ponds, including much of this area, which is actually called Kingswood. I'm serious about the fish, too. There are stories of people fishing koi carp and huge goldfish out of their gardens when the waters finally began to subside, which had presumably been washed out of garden ponds or local parks before they were able to enjoy a rather brief though an ultimately fatal spell of freedom swimming around road signs and beneath cars and the like, probably wondering what on earth was going on and pondering why nobody had fed them that day.

There were more dog walkers along this stretch, too, though most of them were on the other side of the river where the majority of the houses were, so we still enjoyed relative silence. In the distance, we could just about hear the sounds of traffic, and behind the trees, we could see the bridge that carried the road over the river not too far ahead of us.

We were soon at this bridge, and a small

tunnel led us beneath it. This was the first bridge we had seen along this little river, although technically it is two bridges, not that you can tell from underneath.

There should, by all rights, not be a bridge here at all, as the original plans had envisioned a road tunnel beneath the river, which engineers started to build in 1993. Unfortunately, the engineers in question were pretty rubbish, as their tunnel kept flooding, so eventually, they gave up, filled it in with rubble and built the bridges instead.

On that note, this is where we gave up. The temptation was too strong, as we were only a mile or so from my house, and although it wasn't all that late, I suggested to Rob that we wouldn't have time to finish the walk today after all, and anyway, we didn't want to rush it.

Instead, we veered off and headed home, and this next bit was perhaps the oddest walk I had ever been on. While I have walked through urban areas carrying my backpack many times, walking through my own backyard, so to speak, was an altogether different and somewhat strange experience. I almost felt overdressed, and for a moment or two, I was concerned that I would bump into somebody I knew, and they would presume me to have gone insane, wandering down my own street dressed as if I was backpacking through the Serengeti.

Nonetheless, this feeling only lasted a second or two, after which I decided that I didn't care and that if I did bump into anyone I knew, I would simply tell them I had gone insane and that I was indeed very much enjoying backpacking through the Serengeti.

A North East Coast Town

To Hull And Back

Just a couple of days passed, and after having somehow persuaded Rob to pull a sickie so we could finally finish this walk, we met exactly where we left off, at the double bridge over the mighty River Hull. A somewhat cooler day greeted us, though we didn't care because we knew we would soon warm up once we got moving.

It's probably a good job that I'm out walking today, too. For reasons that are not important, while my wife was drying the pots this morning, she told me that I didn't have a sense of humour. When I replied that I did and that I could prove it, she looked at me suspiciously. But when I said that I could prove that I had a sense of humour simply by the fact that I had married her, well, let's just say it's a good job that it was a spoon she was drying and not a knife.

Anyway, today would introduce us to a side of our own city that we had never really seen. It really is true that you often fail to appreciate what is right on your own doorstep, and I, like many others, am equally guilty of this when it comes to my home city.

Hull, you see, is an undiscovered gem. Part of me is even reluctant to put this down on paper, as many, many people have a somewhat negative image of the city, which is fine by me, as it keeps those pesky tourists away.

If you live somewhere like York, Chester or Bath, you will know exactly what I mean. Every April, usually starting sometime around Easter, hordes of crazy tourists begin to descend on many of our most beautiful towns and cities, clogging the streets and pushing up prices, a plague which usually lasts until around the end of September.

Not so in Hull, thank you very much. The place stays pretty much quiet all year round, which is exactly how I, and around another two hundred thousand other wise people, want it to remain. So, whatever you do, please don't ever tell anyone if you ever wake up one morning and suddenly discover that you think, on reflection, Hull is really rather bloody nice. The neighbours would kill me.

I told Rob that we had a day of learning ahead of us, that we were going to find out things about our own city that would both amaze and confound us both, and that by the end of the day, we would be awash with fascinating facts and sensational snippets, but he just picked his fingernails and ignored me, so I wandered off along the riverbank hoping he would follow.

He did, which meant we were both soon deep in a cloud of midges that seemed to rather enjoy living on this particular bit of real estate. I don't blame them either, as there was easy access to water, lots of food in the form of walkers and ramblers, and also rather nice views.

Hull has a longer history than you might possibly expect, I said to Rob. It was first established by some rather brave monks from Meaux Abbey sometime in the 12th century. They farmed sheep and shipped wool along the Humber to more profitable markets, and in 1293 the town became the property of the king, Edward I, and is why it became Kingston Upon Hull, as it was the king's town.

The place sizzled away quietly for a few hundred years and did not really attract much attention until that is, one fateful day in 1642. The king of the day, Charles I, turned up at the city gate and asked very nicely if he could come in and take all the lovely weapons that were stored in the town. After a meeting to decide whether or not he could come in, which in true Hull style was held in the local pub, the city fathers decided that they didn't really want to let him in after all, so the governor, Sir John Hotham, basically told the king and his barmy army to buzz off.

The monarch, not surprisingly, was not very happy at this turn of events, so he laid siege to the city for the next three weeks. This basically started the civil war, which strangely is not something the city shouts about all that much, which is a shame. What is also a shame is that Hotham, although he escaped the city to his manor house in Scorborough, was later captured, thrown in the Tower of London, and eventually executed.

Anyway, it was time to move on. As we headed south following the still twisting river, there was a shopping park on our left that had everything you could possibly desire if you perhaps fancied blowing your entire wage packet one Saturday afternoon. You could, for instance, go watch a movie or perhaps have a game of bowling. If you didn't fancy that, there was a rather classy looking gym where you could attempt to give yourself a heart attack instead. You could then move on to one of the many fine, and some not so fine, eateries, which is perhaps a good time to confess that Rob and myself had briefly grabbed a sausage and egg McMuffin from you know where.

Incidentally, the staff in there are more creative than you think. One of my friends once asked me to check over a job application for them. In the *previous jobs* section, under duties, she had written *handling financial transactions for a multinational company*, which, you have to admit, is a rather clever and incredibly creative way of telling someone that you work on a till in McDonald's.

Anyway, after your food, you could move on to the shops, alternately raiding supermarkets, sports shops, and shoe shops, as well as a particularly nice branch of Next, complete with one of those upmarket restaurants run by one celebrity chef or another who will happily make you a mixed leaf salad in return for half a day's pay. If you did partake in such an act of lunacy, then you would probably find yourself feeling a bit sick when you get the bill, but don't worry, there's a rather large pharmacy here as well where you can grab something to make you feel better or perhaps put yourself to sleep for a few hours to numb the pain.

I'll be honest with you, shopping is my worst nightmare, and quite frankly, I would rather stick bamboo shards up my nose than spend a day at one of these places, but each to their own,

I guess.

Houses stood on our right, though once again, I found myself wondering about the wisdom of living in one of them, as they appeared to have been built below sea level, or more accurately, river level. In fact, when I got in touch with the local water authority, one chirpy chappy cheerfully told me that 90% of Hull was, in fact, below sea level. He went on to remind me, as if I needed reminding, that Hull is actually ranked the second most vulnerable city for flooding after London, which explains why my house insurance has been so high. The city, you see, suffered great flooding in both 2007 and 2013, in what were both said to be a once in a century flood, which simply tells us that somebody can't count when you think about it.

He also told me to imagine Hull as a bowl, which puzzled me for a moment and made me wonder if I should perhaps ingest some hallucinogenic mushrooms or snort on some pepper. In actual fact, after a moment of clarity, I decided that it is actually pretty easy to imagine Hull as a bowl, as it is more or less flat. The edges are the important thing, said Chris, my new best friend at Yorkshire Water, with higher edges to the north which go on to become the Yorkshire Wolds, and the frontages along the Humber which were built by the Vikings forming the protective barrier to the south against the

Humber estuary.

I digested that for a second or ten and then asked for clarification, and Chris said that, yes, the major part of the defences of the city were actually built by the Vikings over a thousand years ago, and their work is still largely what protects us today, which is just mad, I said to Rob, and is something that neither of us knew or even suspected. I still wouldn't live in these houses, though.

We shuffled on through the clouds of midges, passing a rather large reservoir to our left that seemed to be home to a lone heron, which was unexpected. Initially, he just stood there staring at us from the opposite bank, but when we clearly became too close for comfort, which wasn't actually all that close, he took flight, flapping his enormous wings ever so gracefully and somewhat slowly, which made the fact that he actually managed to take off even more amazing than it already was.

The houses petered out and were replaced by trees, behind which was an old manor house of some kind. This was Haworth Hall, and I have fond memories of coming here in my youth with many of my friends and sneaking around in the woods playing various games. The house was still lived in at the time, and I remember being caught by the butler after we had sneaked in one afternoon. He never caught us, though, the old slowcoach, and we thought we had gotten away with it until I arrived home and got a clip around the head. Apparently, he had recognised one of us and had made a phone call, after which that parent had phoned another who had phoned another and so on. After that, we never told our parents the whole truth about who we were playing out with, and we never got caught again.

One of the things I remember about playing out around here was that many of the houses still had air raid shelters, even though the war was a distant memory even when I was young. There are not many to be seen nowadays, though there are one or two, and they are generally square concrete structures with walls that must have been around 12 inches thick.

This was good because as well as being the second most risky city for flooding after London, it is often said that Hull was the second most bombed city after London when taking in size and population. For security reasons, though, and so as not to let those nasty Nazis know how good a job they were doing, which was a pretty good one, this was kept well under wraps. As we heard earlier, Hull was often side-lined in the press and simply referred to as a north east coast town that had been bombed, though in reality, the place was more or less flattened.

During the war, the city suffered more than 80 air raids, with the bulk being between May and July 1941, which became known as the Hull Blitz. On the evening of Wednesday 7th May alone, over 90 Nazi bombers dropped in excess of 9,000 incendiary bombs on Hull, which explains why so many children ended up being evacuated to Beverley. But this wasn't the worst of it. The next night, around 120 bombers returned and dropped a further 20,000 bombs in one night, which is a staggering number, especially considering that Hull is such a small city.

By Friday morning, much of the city was on fire, but there were some exceptional stories that came out of this, and rather amazingly and no matter how unlikely, one of them involved none other than William Wilberforce, though I will save that for later.

Anyway, by the end of the blitz on the city, it literally stood in ruins. Being a resident of the place myself, I am therefore wholly qualified and quite allowed to say that this is why so many of our buildings are not what you might call beautiful. This certainly helps to explain why some people are not all that fond of the place, though I will forgive them for their ignorance, as they are probably not aware that the city was generously re-modelled by the Nazis in the early 1940s. Of the 92,000 houses in the city, only 6,000 remained undamaged by the end of the war, which had ultimately seen the deaths of 1,200 people, with over 150,000 made homeless, a truly staggering figure which represented most of the city's population. Sad times indeed.

We moved on along the curves of the river and caught a glimpse of a tall building in the distance. This was the library of Hull University, and it is a building I am very familiar with. I spent many evenings there cramming for exams, usually when I belatedly realised that I had forgotten to actually revise and the exams in question were just 72 short hours away. It wasn't just me, though, and the library usually became something of a hive of activity around these times, but otherwise generally resembled the Mary Celeste, with not a soul to be seen from floor to floor. Interestingly, the building I spent most of my time in was actually the Wilberforce Building, home to the politics department, and was named after William Wilberforce too. The city simply loves him, it seems.

The university, and specifically the library, also once had a rather notable resident. Famous poet Philip Larkin spent 30 years here after taking a job as the university's head librarian in 1955. There is a larger-than-life statue of him in the train station for all who arrive at the end of the line that is Hull, and it is during his stay that he wrote much of his best work. The city has since embraced him as one of their own, however, the people of Hull, of whom I am one, of course, might not like the next bit. It is said, you see, that Larkin, was actually not all that fond of the place. Or its peoples.

Just a month after taking up his job in the city, he was already deriding the place as well as the Hullensians, which is what we are called, apparently, though some people call us codheads. He wrote a letter to his good chum and fellow poet Dennis Enright with a very polite put-down, stating, *'I'm settling down alright, every day I sink a little further.'*

A month later, his insults had become slightly more direct, so much so that even the thickest among us might be able to spot them, especially when he wrote, *'what a hole, what a witless, crapulous people'.*

He even invented a new word – crapulous, which I rather like, and I fully intend to use it at every possible opportunity, I told Rob.

He also told other people, again through his letters, that the place smelled of fish and was a dump, and as a native of the place myself, I can confirm that, at the time, this was indeed true. Don't worry, though, as the fish industry has since collapsed, and while this has caused the odd problem, such as the slight inconvenience of thousands of job losses and the utter destruction of the communities within which these lovely people lived as well as severe financial and economic problems, at least the city doesn't stink anymore. Well, not of fish, anyway.

Perhaps his best insult to the city, though, was when he wrote to Enright saying, '*I wish I could think of just one nice thing to tell you about Hull - oh yes, well, it's very nice and flat for cycling.*'

Ouch. That hurts.

But the truth is that Larkin really did like Hull, referring to it as his lonely northern daughter, and he spoke favourably of the unpretentiousness of both the people and the city and put it on record that it had less '*crap around*' than London, which we'll take as a compliment, thank you very much. And at least it's not Bradford, I said to Rob as we moved on.

We came to a main road which we dodged across in style and grace just next to Sutton Road bridge, which is not much to look at though it does have a sense of humour. Way back in 2020, on the 11th of February, to be exact, the bridge opened on its own and without warning, presumably surprising those who were trying to drive across it. Luckily, nobody died, but regardless, I no longer trust this bridge and give it my most evil eye every time I drive across it, which is most days. It does have rather nice wigwags, though. Don't worry, I didn't know what wigwags were either until I started looking into this haunted bridge. Wigwags are actually the flashing lights you see at such places as bridges, railroad crossings and strip clubs, and I, for one, think wigwags is an awesome name. It would have made a great name for one of my kids. Oh, and by the way, if you're wondering how I know that strip clubs have them, a friend of a friend of a friend told me, honest.

As I said, we crossed the road here, much to the annoyance of the delivery truck driver, who clearly thought that he didn't have to slow down, never mind stop, and was not happy when he was forced to do so. This is probably because when I say style and grace, what I actually mean is waddled and shuffled, as we had mistimed our crossing and had failed to take into consideration the fact that we were carrying rather large rucksacks and therefore were not able to move as swiftly as perhaps we might normally have done.

We carried on along the riverbank on the other side of this road, deep in conversation about one or another very silly subject, so we did not realise that we should have actually crossed to the other side of the river, which meant we had to double back after a few hundred yards.

Getting back to the bridge at Ennerdale, which was of a much older type than the previous bridge, I was reminded of some nasty horses that lived along the riverbank, which is the real reason why I had brought my walking poles. The last time I had been up here, admittedly some time ago, I had been with my wife, who had foolishly volunteered to come on one of these silly walks. We had gone maybe half a mile or so, which was when we came to the horses, and while the first couple of them had been fine, the third one had decided he was going to be a bit of a cretin.

While I don't normally call animals names, this one definitely deserved it. He first approached us, initially quite calmly, but had, at the last minute, decided that we should go for a swim in the river. To facilitate this, he tried to knock us with his head at the same time as forcing us backwards towards the water with the huge mass of his body. I'm not sure if you've ever been attacked by a horse, but it's surprisingly scary, and it was only because he was tied to a chain that saved us. I must admit, I did feel a touch of glee as he momentarily strangled himself, and I was almost tempted to laugh, but I decided not to, just in case this just made him angrier still.

Unfortunately, his mates, who had up until then been munching happily on some soggy grass, decided that they wanted a bit of the action too, which necessitated going even closer to the water's edge, much to the annoyance of Mrs Amess. Needless to say, she has not been for a walk with me since and, in fact, scoffs at any suggestion of such madness.

There were no horses today, though. Someone from the council had stuck a sign onto the fence, which we had not initially noticed when we had first passed the bridge and which we only read as we now doubled back to cross it. To cut a long story short, the council had said that any horses left tied up on this riverbank would be removed at the beginning of April, and as we were now very much past that date, hey presto, they were gone. I was initially very happy about this, but my euphoria soon disappeared when I read the rest of the notice. The horses, you see, would be removed and disposed of, which sounds, quite frankly, distinctly like they would be turned into glue or maybe dog food. On a positive note, at least they wouldn't bother me anymore.

After crossing the river, we continued on our correct course and found ourselves in a much more industrial environment. Factories lined our left, and a huge wind turbine towered above us, spinning slowly but steadily.

We passed some kind of training centre that had what looked like a helicopter parked outside, but on closer inspection, it was only half a helicopter, presumably used for survival training.

On the opposite bank, large claws ripped cars apart, stripping and smashing them into shreds, which was pretty cool to watch for a moment or two until we realised the dust we were breathing in was probably not all that good for us.

The path was still easy to walk along, but it was beginning to get somewhat overgrown, indicating that not as many people walked along this section as on the others, which was not surprising given the industrial nature of the area. Still, it was interesting to see.

The river continued to snake its way through the city, and we followed it obediently along, eventually coming to two modern bridges that were more or less clones of the two we had seen at the shopping park as we first came into Hull.

There was no tunnel here, though, so we had to cross an incredibly busy road, but luckily, the traffic was gridlocked, as it usually is in Hull, which meant there was no risk of being squished. The motorists all looked rather miserable, which was not because they were sitting in traffic, but was actually due to the fact that they couldn't squish us, suggested Rob.

The industrial nature of the buildings continued, and we even saw traces of train tracks just after the bridges. Their orientation indicated that there must have been a railway bridge across the river here at some point in the past, but nowadays, there was just mud and an old shopping trolley.

We were about to leave the river behind, so we said our goodbyes and climbed up a small footbridge, though the bridge in question never took us over the river but took us in the opposite direction. Strangely, however, the bridge never crossed anything, so we stopped at the top to try and figure out why it was there.

I grew up around here, and I can vaguely remember some kind of facility here, and although I had no idea what it had been, it had consisted of thousands of pipes. The footbridge must have originally taken walkers over whatever these pipes had been, but it now crossed nothing. Below us, we could see yet another machine ripping apart some kind of metal construction, though there was not much left, and I suggested to Rob that in a few weeks or months, all traces of whatever had been here would be gone forever, and it would probably be replaced with yet another shopping park, he added.

We now headed east, but only for a few hundred yards, so we could join up with another disused railway line. This one would take us towards the town centre, and was a delight to walk along. The occasional cyclist passed us by, but other than that, we had the path to ourselves. Well, ourselves and around a thousand noisy sparrows and a rather scary squirrel.

We passed a football field which today was full of lots of young kids playing the glorious game. None of them probably knew that Hull is linked to the game in a rather curious way, for Hull was the home and birthplace of a young man called Ebeneezer Cobb Morley.

If you like football, then you actually have much to thank him for, as he was heavily involved in the creation of the Football Association as well as the rules of football and was later known as the father of English football, although it is probably fair to say that we are still arguing about the offside rule even after all these years, so he didn't get everything right. Regardless, his book *Laws of Football* is regarded by many as one of the most influential books ever, right up there with the likes of *The Bible* and *On the Origin of the Species*.

He even played in the first official match in 1863, which was used to test the new laws, after which they became much more widely adopted. Quite bizarrely, before the rules came into being, players could often be seen running towards the goal while actually holding the ball, which basically sounds a lot like rugby when you think about it. Shin kicking was also allowed, a practice that was called hacking and was something that almost became a part of the modern game. At a vote to decide whether or not to allow it, it was only decided not to because some of those who supported it failed to turn up at this crucial meeting.

Cobb was born in Hull but moved to London

as a young man to pursue his career as a solicitor. Curiously, the house where he lived in Richmond-upon-Thames in London was later to be the home of pop star Duffy, and even more curiously, this house collapsed like a deck of cards during renovation work in 2015 which aimed to extend the basement, which was perhaps not wise as the house was only a few metres from the River Thames, something that was said to have possibly contributed to the collapse. No shit, Sherlock.

Moving on, we crossed another road, turned a corner, and went under an underpass, all the while chatting away about this and that, barely noticing the world around us. Until that is, we came across a huge building that had more security than Fort Knox, by the looks of it. I didn't know what it was at the time, and they had no signs up, but I later found out that it was a production facility for Reckitt Benckiser, hence the electric fences and razor wire, as well as bollards and gates that protected whatever it was they were cooking up in there.

Hull has actually given the world quite a lot, which Rob and myself had been discussing as we went along, so before we go on, we should take a moment to find out exactly what this little smartie of a town has given us.

There are countless people to mention, for instance, it was local native Christopher Langton who invented the scanner that tests us oldies for osteoporosis, and for which I am personally very grateful. How about John Hall, who is virtually unknown even within the city. Hall emigrated to New Zealand and, to cut a long story short, eventually became Prime Minister down there. He was very interested in women's rights and led a parliamentary campaign for women's suffrage, resulting in New Zealand becoming the first country in the world to give women the vote. You're welcome, ladies.

David Whitfield was also born and raised here. His biggest hit was *'Cara Mia'* in 1954, which made him the first British male singer to earn a gold disc for one million record sales in the UK, and the first British artist to enter the US Top Ten. Hull would probably shout about him a bit more than it does if it wasn't for one tiny detail. In October 1966, he was found guilty of exposing himself to two young girls, and let's just say that was the end of his career.

You can also thank us for the amazing music of Paul Heaton and Jackie Abbott and their bands, *The Housemartins* and *The Beautiful South*. Maureen Lipman was born here too, and chemist George Gray had a long career at Hull University, playing around with liquid crystals and eventually coming up with the LCD display. Without him, then, those of you reading this on a flat screen would instead find yourselves holding an actual book, and that thing hanging from your wall that you call a television would still be a ridiculously big square box taking up most of the corner of your living room.

I'm going to have to tell myself off for what I have just done, as I have, in fact, just found myself guilty of using a redundant acronym. I apologise profusely, as it is well documented that LCD stands for liquid crystal display, and therefore my use of the word display after LCD is wholly unwarranted, unforgivable and downright rude, to put it mildly.

Don't get me wrong, I'm not a grammar Nazi, but I do get annoyed when I hear people using redundant acronyms, so I try not to do it myself. I am sometimes as guilty as anybody else when it comes to this, however, and I regularly use the phrase pin number, for instance, which is silly, as pin already stands for personal identification number.

Furthermore, ATM machine is another one I am guilty of using, with ATM already standing for automated teller machine anyway, and VIN number is another of my favourites, meaning vehicle identification number. DC Comics is pointless, as DC stands for Detective Comics, but the most common of all has to be what is usually on the bottom of a wedding invite - Please RSVP - Please Répondez s'il vous plaît - which translates to Please Respond Please. Incidentally, I recently received a wedding invitation from someone I don't particularly like. I replied *maybe next time*.

Face-punching former deputy Prime Minister John Prescott, who famously smacked egg-throwing protestor, Craig Evans, right in the face with a mean left hook, also made Hull his lifelong home and spent many years as the Member of Parliament for the city. He was good entertainment value too, at least as far as MPs go, and was often in the news, though not always for the right reasons. Not many places can claim to have a Member of Parliament that can smack voters and get away with it.

There must be something in the water here, as Prezza is not the first of our MPs to bash his constituents up a little. In fact, the first one was none other than William Wilberforce. While on the campaign trail in 1780, someone threw a stone at him. Bizarrely, Wilberforce's butcher, a man named Johnny Bell, managed to discover the identity of the miscreant. It was recorded at the time that Bell went to Wilberforce and promised to kill the culprit that same night, to which Wilberforce replied, *'no, don't kill him, just scare him a little.'* Ah, Hull, such a wonderful town, and a crucible of democracy too.

Tom Courtenay, Ian Carmichael and John Alderton all hailed from Hull, and more recently, Reece Shearsmith was born here, who starred alongside Steve Pemberton in *The League of Gentlemen*, a surreal British comedy that describes a weird town, somewhat different from the rest of the country, where all the people are a bit odd. I'm not implying anything about Hull there, by the way. I'm just stating the facts.

There is also Jim Radford, a little-known folk singer and peace campaigner who was born in the city in 1928. Radford, it turns out, was also the youngest person who was known to have taken part in the allied invasion of Normandy in 1944, being only fifteen years old at the time. For his bravery, he was awarded the highest order of merit in the French military, *The Legion of Honour*. Sadly, he passed away from COVID-19 in late 2020, aged 92 years young.

Joseph Arthur Rank was also born here, and without him, it is doubtful that Britain would have the flourishing film industry that it enjoys today. His first film was called *Turn of the Tide*, which he made easily enough, though he encountered problems when it came to distribution, which was mainly dominated by American companies. To get around this, Rank was forced to invest in both distribution and exhibition, effectively creating Pinewood Studios from scratch in 1935 and buying the Odeon Cinema chain in 1938, all so he could show his movies to the public.

Rank went on to make some of the best-known movies of his day, including *A Night to*

Remember, which told the story of the Titanic, as well as *Victim*, which was the first British film to use the word 'homosexual' and which told the story of a gay man being played by Dirk Bogarde who sets out to find those who are trying to destroy his life. And if those both sound a bit dark, Rank also made all of those wonderful Norman Wisdom films that became so famous and which inadvertently and quite unexpectedly made Wisdom something of a god behind the Iron Curtain in general and Albania in particular.

Also on a film note, Gerald Thomas came from Hull, and if you have not heard of him, it is he who directed all, and I mean all, of the *Carry On* films, starting with *Carry On Sargeant* in 1958 right up until the somewhat belated last movie, *Carry On Colombus* in 1992.

Furthermore, the boiled sweet was invented in Hull, courtesy of Needlers, and the city was also the birthplace of Lemsip, Bonjela and Gaviscon, all invented at Reckitt Benckiser, not far from where we were currently standing, of course.

On the flip side, Hull has often been picked out as being perhaps not the best place to live. In 2015, it featured on the list of a well-known website as being the second-worst place to live in the country, coming in at a shameful 137th place, with Edinburgh coming in as the nicest place to live in 1st position. The only saving grace, perhaps, is that Bradford came in at 138th place, though in reality, this is not really saying much, is it? And, in fact, it rather annoys me that Bradford beat us, so to speak, if I am really telling the truth.

Compounding this even further, Hull is also regularly featured in the Crap Towns series of books, which is fine by me, as anything that keeps people away helps us to keep our dirty little secret, in that Hull is actually quite alright, but once again, please don't tell anyone I said that.

I justify this by an experience I had in York a few years back. One of my children was living there whilst studying at the city's university, and I had met him for lunch one sunny spring day. I can distinctly remember simultaneously finding out what it is like to be a sardine and also what it is like for a salmon trying to swim upstream. A throng of tourists surrounded us at every instance, and all of the cafes were full wherever we went. On top of this, they had all increased their prices in order to rip off said tourists, so as I said, keeping Hull a well-kept secret is fine by me and telling would-be visitors that the place is a crapulous hole is an absolutely fantastic idea.

There's another reason that I don't particularly want tourists clogging up the place. Tourists, by definition, tend to come from faraway lands, and, pray tell, what do faraway lands have? Things like COVID-19, SARS and Monkeypox. Think about it, my friends, think about it.

The city also gave the world the first-ever submarium. It has sharks and fish and lobsters and loads of other wet things that swim, as well as some rather comical penguins, and while some more cynical types out there would argue that a submarium is, in fact, simply an aquarium going sneakily by another name, to them, I would stick my tongue out and blow them a big fat rasparium.

While we had been talking about all of this, we had carried on ambling slowly along the railway line, before turning off and heading towards the city centre.

We crossed another bridge, North Bridge, which appeared to be a clone of the older type we had seen at Ennerdale, and saw yet another more or less identical bridge to our left, which was Drypool Bridge. Drypool Bridge, like Sutton Road Bridge, also tends to randomly open on its own every now and then and has, in fact, done so on several occasions when pedestrians, cars, and even buses have been crossing it. Such incidents as this are exactly the reason I always wear clean underwear, just in case I end up in the hospital from some freakishly unlikely incident or accident, such as attempted murder by a bridge. And while we're on this subject, never do anything you couldn't see yourself explaining to a paramedic, just in case, which, let's face it, is very good life advice indeed.

Incidentally, Drypool Bridge is painted with Venn diagrams, though I will explain why in a moment or two.

We wandered on, and we actually left the official route of our walk. A small diversion is needed, you see, as the Wilberforce Way, for some unfathomable reason, fails to take in the Wilberforce Monument, which is but a hop, skip and a jump from the course of the route. It is quite an impressive monument, too, being a column of 90 feet in height, topped by a larger-than-life statue of Wilberforce himself. Look carefully, and in his hand, you can even see a scroll, which represents the abolition act that he fought so long and hard for.

We are lucky to have it, as the column was nearly never built. To say there was a bit of rivalry between Hull and York would be an understatement, as both towns claimed Wilberforce as their own, and both thought they alone would be best placed to commemorate him after his death, and this rivalry would simultaneously help and hinder the Hull column.

Pivotal to the point of actually getting the statue built was a man of the cloth called the Reverend Henry Venn. Incidentally, he was the father of Sir John Venn, the inventor of the

Venn diagram, which are those fancy diagrams that show relationships between various things by the use of overlapping circles, and which was another gift from Hull to the world and which explains the fancy paintwork we saw on Drypool Bridge.

Anyway, Henry Venn was the one who came up with the idea of a large monument, something that was not all that common at the time. Others had suggested a memorial in the church or perhaps a school for the poor, but when Venn lobbied for something big and bold that all visitors to the city would be unable to miss, everyone else soon fell into line behind him.

Thus, just a year after his death, the huge column went up right in the heart of the city, just near the dock offices, though there was an issue with funding, which dried up for a while when people instead chose to donate to the idea of a school for the blind in York instead.

Originally, the idea was to build just the column, but the project was changed to include a statue of Wilberforce on top partly to get one over on those scallywags in York and their rather feeble attempt to honour Wilberforce with their poxy school.

To cut a long story short, the column and statue were fully finished by 1835, just two years after Wilberforce had passed away, and it still stands to this very day, though it was moved to its present location in front of the college in 1935, exactly a hundred years after it first went up. This was because, in its original position, the monument had become something of an impediment at what was, by then, one of the busiest road junctions in Hull.

And as for York and their feeble school, well, that closed in 1958 and is now long gone and forgotten by more or less everyone apart from history nerds.

And finally, and I do apologise for this, but there is something I need to tell you about the statue that my young son pointed out. If you stand at the correct angle and in the right place below the statue, the scroll in his hand looks like his willy. I think it is time to move on, don't you?

Queens Gardens was next, just across the road from the Wilberforce Willy, and we were looking for something to commemorate the time when this beautiful garden was Queens Dock, and which was where fictional literary character Robinson Crusoe sailed from before being stranded on a desert island for the best part of 28 years, encountering cannibals and captives along the way, as immortalised in the famous book by Daniel Defoe.

Evidently, perhaps like Larkin, Defoe didn't

think too much of Hull, and in a book describing his tour of Britain, he remarked:

'From Beverley I came to Hull, a distance 6 miles. If you would expect me to give an account of . . . any of the second-rate cities abroad . . . the town of Hull may be a specimen.'

Not exactly high praise, is it? This is probably why he chose it as the departure point for his famous literary character Robinson Crusoe, who set sail from here in what is now a classic piece of British literature, and who actually came from York. In the book, the full title of which was a then-fashionable sixty-five words long but which is now commonly just called Robinson Crusoe, he is said to have sailed from Queen's Dock in 1651, which was not only clever but probably involved magic, as the dock wasn't built until 1778, but Defoe was never one to let facts get in the way. Regardless, there is a plaque in Queen's Gardens to commemorate Crusoe, as the dock was filled in after it closed in 1930 and has since become a public park.

Defoe redeemed himself later, however, when he said of Crusoe, *'Had I the sense to return to Hull, I had been happy,'* which suggests it can't be that bad, after all then, but maybe anywhere is better than a desert island? Anyway, to his credit, he certainly never called the people crapulous. I told you I liked that word.

We looked all over the park trying to find the plaque but were out of luck, which was, quite frankly, a bit crapulous.

While we were off-piste, so to say, and not on the actual route of the Wilberforce Way, we decided to take in a few more sights of Hull, all of which were within a few minutes walk.

The first stop was perhaps one of the more unusual names for a street, and that was the *Land of Green Ginger*. Nobody really knows why this street has such an odd and simultaneously wonderful name, and there are various competing explanations, including the fact that an exotic spice called green ginger may once have been imported through here from the nearby docks on the River Hull, or it may have possibly come from a Dutch family called the Lindegreen's who once lived here.

Perhaps the highlight of a wander down this little lane, though, is England's smallest window, situated in the wall of the George pub. To be honest, a first glance gives you the impression that the builders simply forgot to put any cement in between two of the bricks, but a closer examination reveals the actual window, and a nice brass plaque tells its story.

We also had a quick look in an old pub with the even older name of Ye Olde White Hart, which was built in 1550 and is the pub we mentioned earlier where the decision to refuse the king entry into the city was actually made, even before the king had arrived, apparently. This difficult decision was finalised upstairs by the townspeople on the 23rd of April in a room that is now known as the Plotting Parlour, and there is also a human skull behind the bar for all to see, which was found there following a fire in the 19th century.

Monument Bridge was next, where we stumbled across Beverley Gate, which was once the entrance to the walled city but is nowadays more of a hole in the ground. Don't be fooled, though, as it would once have been just as impressive as the gate we passed at North Bar in Beverley, and in fact, this site is of considerable historical significance as it is considered by many to be the exact spot where the English Civil War started, as well as, if you remember, where Sir Robert Constable was hanged by Henry VIII.

It was April 1642, and this is the actual spot where, as we heard earlier, King Charles demanded access to the city and, therefore, to the large cache of weapons and ammunition stored within its walls. Parliament had beaten him to it, however, having appointed Sir John Hotham as the Governor of Hull, and had given him specific instructions not to surrender the town to the king. As has already been mentioned, Hotham's refusal to allow the king into the town, therefore, became the first act of defiance of the civil war, and the king was forced to move on to Beverley, where he set up camp and decided to put Hull under siege and to make the town pay for its insolence.

Fast forward to July, when the king made his move on Hull, and he found his forces repelled by the Parliamentarians holding the city, an act which became the first actual military confrontation of the war. The king was unsuccessful, however, and by the end of July, he was forced to abandon his designs on the city and moved on in defeat, which, unlikely as it may sound, brings us to telephone boxes.

You may have already noticed that Hull's telephone boxes are different from others in the country in that they are cream as opposed to red, but this is not the only difference. If you take a closer look at the top of a standard British phone box, you will see a crown which pays tribute to the king or queen of the day. However, if you take a look at one of the cream-coloured Hull phone boxes, there is no crown, which is a direct reference to the city's defiance towards the royals during the civil war, which some say is disrespectful, but to me, it is just funny that anybody cares about such trivia

A shop nearby was selling newspapers, and like most towns and cities, Hull has its own local daily rag, which has, over the years, printed some corkers of a story. One of my favourites concerned events in the city of October the 8th, 1948, which described an interesting morning at an undertaker's office. At 11.30am prompt, a monkey walked into the undertaker's but immediately made a hurried exit before climbing up a tree and disappearing. No context is given for this story, and there was seemingly no follow up, not that I could find at least, so it will just have to remain one of life's little mysteries. Regardless, I find it hard to think of whatever series of events that led to a monkey wandering randomly into an undertaker's in the north of England, but there you go. It was in the paper, so it must be true.

Part of me wonders if my family were responsible for this story, as, after the war, my grandad travelled the world and once brought back a small monkey. It was, in his own words, a vicious little shit, and it took a particular disliking to one of his cousins, and every time she came to visit, it would try to rip her scalp off. He never mentioned an undertaker's, though, but I am told it did escape on more than one occasion, so you never know.

Another interesting article described how a gentleman reported an incident of bullying to the police in 1922. Apparently, children kept running up to him and shouting *beaver*, a reference to his beard, something which was quite common back then. The man told police that he didn't see anything funny about running up to someone and shouting beaver, but nonetheless, after this was published in the newspaper, the number of similar incidents skyrocketed for several weeks, which is not surprising. We should try this ourselves, I mention to Rob.

Perhaps the favourite headline to catch my attention, however, was *Second Scorpion Found in Man's Bedroom*. I must admit it was the word *second* that grabbed my attention, and although there was no real explanation given, you can only presume that perhaps he lived above a pet shop. Anyway, the man said that during the first incident a couple of years back, he had simply screamed, at which point his wife came in and squashed it with a brick, though why she happened to have a brick in her hand raises more questions than it answers. All I can offer is that she was from Hull. On the second occasion, however, he was alone and naked, which raises yet more questions, as his wife had since left him, though I'm not surprised, considering he was such a pansy. Anyway, wondering what to do with this second visitor, he decided to stand on it. He maybe wasn't of the biggest brain, and you can probably guess what happened next, and you would be right.

There are lots of statues in Hull, but two stand

out distinctly, and one is of Queen Victoria, just behind us. The other is of William of Orange, or King Billy as he is affectionately called locally. It's not actually the statues themselves that cause me to mention them, but it is their placement.

You see, the people of Hull, with their long-running feud with royalty that obviously goes back to the civil war and which has caused them to paint their phone boxes cream and refuse to put little crowns on them, has also caused them to also put both of these statues of the monarchy on top of a Hull toilet. Make of that what you will. And while we are talking about King Billy, this is the king that was killed by a mole when his horse put its foot into a molehill, thus changing the course of English history. He broke his collarbone in the fall, developed pneumonia, and was soon as dead as a doornail, but not before he introduced gin to Britain, something for which my wife is eternally grateful, I imagine. Still, as deaths go, it was a bit of a silly one.

We wandered down to yet another statue, this one of famous aviator Amy Johnson. Perhaps Hull's most famous daughter, Johnson became famous as the first woman to fly solo from England to Australia in 1930. She had aimed to set a new record for this trip, which she didn't quite manage, though she became somewhat famous nonetheless.

Mystery surrounds her death. She had been

delivering a plane from Blackpool to Oxfordshire yet somehow ended up many miles off course, had managed to fly to the wrong side of London, and was last seen over the River Thames, where witnesses claimed to have seen either the wreckage of her aircraft or her body in the water.

Although she had supposedly been flying alone, another body was also seen in the water. In 1999, reports emerged suggesting that she had been shot down by friendly fire, while another account claims she was sucked into the ship's propellers, and there has even been some speculation that she was on a secret mission. Her body and aircraft were never recovered, and at least one man died attempting to rescue her, although her flight bag containing a few of her possessions did wash up on a nearby beach a few days later.

We had one more stop to make before carrying on with our walk, and that was the train station. It made perfect sense to call in there, not least because we had spent a good deal of this walk following disused railway lines, but also because it has a history in its own right. Built by George Hudson, the Railway King we have already met once or twice, it was initially called Hudson's Folly because of its monumental size, as at the time of its construction, it was the largest in England, and let's be honest, this is Hull and not that many people come here.

That was not always the case, though. In the late 1800s, it is estimated that over two million emigrants passed through here on their way to America. A special platform was even built outside of the main station building, which is still there but is no longer used. The idea was to keep the emigrants away from the regular station users to prevent the spread of disease. They even had their own waiting room, which still exists but is now a pub called *The Tiger's Lair*, in reference to the local football club *Hull City*, which is nicknamed *The Tigers*.

Frustrated at not being able to find the Robinson Crusoe plaque earlier and more or less finished on our little saunter around Hull, we decided to venture back to the park to have another go at finding it. Despite scouring the place from top to bottom for a second time, we finally gave up, as not only was time getting on, but so were we.

We now found ourselves on the last stretch of our walk and headed back to the River Hull, which we would follow for the last half mile, where it would empty into the Humber. Many people call it the River Humber, by the way, but they are stupid, as it is not a river at all. It is actually an estuary, with the difference being that an estuary is basically where the rivers and the tides meet.

Anyway, along the way, and on another

nautical note, a rather famous ship was built in Hull. Blayde's Shipyard saw the launch of a merchant ship named Bethia in 1782, and it is perhaps important to note that she was designed to have a crew of fifteen. While you might not have heard of her, you have probably heard of HMS Bounty, which became her new name when she was bought by the admiralty when she was just five years old; however, the navy, in their wisdom, decided that she could actually accommodate a crew three times as large as she was designed for. This decision might help explain the mutiny that she is now so well known for, which saw most of the crew rebel against the captain, William Bligh.

Bligh was famously set adrift in a boat on the high seas by Fletcher Christian in 1789, partly because the crew of the Bounty wanted to go back to Tahiti and to the many women they had met there. Ultimately, after tossing their captain into a boat and setting him adrift in the middle of the Pacific Ocean, Christian and his crew eventually ended up on Pitcairn Island, one of the most remote in the world, where they set fire to what was left of the Bounty after stripping it of everything useful. It was not a happy ending, though. Most of the sailors ended up slightly dead after fighting with Tahitian men they had brought to the island, probably fighting over the women.

And while there was a persistent rumour that Fletcher Christian had actually faked his own death and had fled back to England, there is no real evidence to support this. Regardless, the story became incredibly well-known, and various stars have played Captain Bligh over the years in movies telling this most interesting story, including Errol Flynn, Clark Gable, Marlon Brando and, most recently, Mel Gibson.

The best movie is undoubtedly the one starring Marlon Brando. Made before the days of computer-generated imagery, the producers commissioned and had built a replica of HMS Bounty in 1960, which was, in fact, the first large vessel ever built for a film production that was based on accurate historical sources. The ship has also since been used in *Pirates of the Caribbean,* which starred Johnny Depp as Captain Jack Sparrow, and later embarked on a world tour, visiting Hull in 2007 as a tribute to the original vessel, and was very popular with visitors. Sadly, however, Bounty will not be appearing in any more movies, as she was lost off the coast of North Carolina during Hurricane Sandy in 2012.

Why do they give hurricanes such lame names like Sandy anyway? This is surely the American equivalent of calling a storm Gladys. I have a solution, though. Name that thing *Hurricane Death Megatron 9000,* and I guarantee people will show that thing respect and won't do such stupid stuff as sail an old ship right through the middle of it, for instance. And just to defend storms for one second, they're not all bad. In fact, personally speaking, I quite like the hurricane season. I can just put anything I don't need out on the balcony, and, well, let's just say problem solved.

Our next stop was another one of the highlights of this walk, which was, of course, the home of William Wilberforce, funnily enough now known as Wilberforce House. It has been a museum since the early 1900s, but it has had one or two close calls, so we are lucky indeed to still have the house in our fair city today.

If you cast your mind back to when I mentioned the bombing raids of the Second World War, this particular house has its very own amazing story of survival to tell. During the heavy bombing, much of which was concentrated around the docks and the city centre, Wilberforce House found itself standing among five warehouses which were all ablaze on both sides of the narrow High Street.

When the fire brigade arrived, one man took control of the situation and was eventually credited with saving the building, and this was John Colletta. He found himself in the area just after midnight along with his heavy pump unit, but unfortunately, the water supply had been knocked out during the bombing. Thinking on his feet, he managed to get hold of another hose from up the road, and recognising the importance of the building, he continually sprayed its walls in order to stop the fire spreading from the adjacent warehouses, which were uncomfortably close and already well ablaze.

The amazing thing is that Colletta wasn't really a fireman, but he was, in fact, a milkman who had just volunteered to help. For his bravery and for saving this house in particular, he was awarded the George Medal, which he donated to the museum after the war and is where it can still be viewed today. We were looking forward to seeing it, but at the gate, someone had put a sign up that said it was closed due to having new central heating installed. I guess they're still a bit touchy about fires, then.

The house also featured in a film called *Amazing Grace*, which told the story of Wilberforce's involvement in abolishing the slave trade. It also depicts slave trader cum abolitionist John Newton, who incidentally wrote the hymn *Amazing Grace,* hence the name of the movie, and it was Newton who later became a huge influence on Wilberforce.

There were other museums here too, and if you ever have the time to kill, I would highly recommend them, although we didn't call into any today. If you do, make sure to seek out

John Robert Mortimer's collection of fossils. Apparently, it rocks.

It was as we left the museums that Rob stumbled on an area of cobblestones. For a minute, I thought he was going to go over and scrape his face along the road, but he just managed to regain his balance. His face went red, and I suggested we stop for a minute, but instead he said he would walk it off, although he had certainly acquired something of a limp when he began moving again.

We did have a quick wander down Scale Lane, as a nifty new bridge crosses the River Hull there, and if you listen carefully, you can hear the tweeting of birds as you cross it. They're not nesting on the bridge, though, and what you can hear is actually an audio recording. I'm not sure why they gave the bridge this feature, but it's fun nonetheless, although I am told it is meant to be calming and soothing, especially to those suffering from gephyrophobia, which apparently is the fear of bridges.

If you're both lucky and brave enough to be on the bridge when a boat passes by, you will also discover that you can stay on it as it swings open, which is a novelty I have certainly never encountered before. Despite hanging around for quite a while, however, there was no sign of a boat today, so we soon moved on.

It is actually said that this bridge was the first of its kind in the world to allow passengers to ride on it as it opened, but I'm always dubious with these claims, so I'll get back to you on that one, and anyway, as we have already heard, people have been doing it on bridges all over Hull for years apparently.

Regardless, it has regularly appeared on lists of the world's most impressive bridges, alongside the likes of the Golden Gate and the Sydney Harbour Bridge, which, however unlikely a fact, is certainly a true one, so there you go.

Leaving the bridge behind, at the end of the High Street, we were treated to the first views of the tidal barrier and, just beyond it, the aquarium known as The Deep, meaning, of course, that we were nearly at the end of our walk.

We headed over to the tidal barrier first, which was built in the 1980s to hopefully put a halt to the regular flooding that had dogged Hull for centuries, and Rob mentioned something called *the city speaks*, which was an art installation that had been put here a while back.

This was not something I had heard of, but Rob went on to explain that there was a microphone here, and if you spoke into it, your words would magically appear on a giant screen high above your head for all to see. While this sounds like a great idea, there was one rather big problem, which in retrospect, should have been slightly obvious. More or less as soon as it opened, it had to be turned off after practically everyone who spoke into it used more or less their full inventory of swear words, which must have been really entertaining for all of the passing traffic but very embarrassing for the creators.

Moving on and almost done, we crossed one last bridge and ventured around the side of The Deep towards the banks of the Humber. We settled on a rather large statue of a shark, which incidentally wasn't built on top of a Hull toilet, but there you go.

Gazing out across the water, we congratulated each other on finishing yet another walk, and I bored Rob with the story of the R-38 airship that had crashed out there in the early 1900s, mainly because I wasn't ready for this particular adventure to finish.

At the time, this incident was one of the worst airship disasters ever, and in fact, it remains so to this very day. On the 24th of August 1921, after completing a test flight, the doomed craft was returning to its base at nearby Howden, where it was due to be handed over to the Americans. This was basically because although we had built it, the country had been more or less bankrupted due to the First World War, so it was deemed too expensive to keep and therefore had to go. At the time of the crash, then, the crew consisted of both British and American personnel.

Thousands of people had been lining the Humber, many of whom witnessed first-hand the unfolding disaster. First of all, the airship buckled in the middle, and then both ends began to sag. A spark inevitably caused the hydrogen fuel to ignite, causing a huge fireball that killed most of those on board and blew out windows over much of Hull. Not surprisingly, this event made headlines internationally, not least because it resulted in the deaths of 44 people. The ship was supposed to be the first of four that would be built, but not surprisingly, all the other orders were cancelled. Part of me wondered if this accident had any bearing on Hilda Lyon going on to invent her famous Lyon shape soon after, but we will never know.

And with that, we were done. The walk was over, and we had made it and once again, and I turned to Rob, who told me which walk he wanted to do next, and it wasn't Offa's Dyke.

Conclusion

This is the first walk we had done in our own backyard, so to speak, and it really had been an enjoyable one. From start to finish, there had been beautiful places along the way, all of which told their own amazing stories.

York had been full of history, obviously, but so too had so many other places along the way. My favourite story was perhaps the flying man of Pocklington, and I often wonder what other obscure histories are out there that we are not aware of.

Well, there is only one way to find out, and that is to get out there and find it, which is fully what we intend to do next.

What our next walk will be, though, or when, is uncertain. It turns out that when Rob tripped, right at the end of our walk, he did some serious damage to his ankle. Although he never broke it, by the end of the day the bruising was black.

A couple of trips to the hospital later, and he was diagnosed with tendon and ligament damage, with the doctors telling him to rest up for a few weeks, though in all honesty Rob was probably just telling me this as he had had enough of me. I'd certainly had enough of him.

In the meantime, I needed something to do, and while I had been looking into the bit about the queen owning the coastline around our tiny little island, my attention turned towards the Yorkshire Coast Path.

What could possibly go wrong?

AFTERWORD

Thank you for taking the time to read this book. I hope you enjoyed reading it as much as I enjoyed walking and writing it.

I take full responsibility for any mistakes made, but if there is something you have read that you really feel needs correcting, please contact me.

The best way to do so is through the contact form on my website at paulamess.co.uk.

Please feel free to look at my other work, some of which is detailed in the following pages. I have spent many years wandering our beautiful little island, finding out lots of obscure and lesser-known stories and histories, and have learned that every single place really does have at least one amazing story to tell.

Once again, thank you.

BOOKS BY THIS AUTHOR

54 Degrees North: A Walk Across England

Coast To Coast: Finding Wainwright's England

All Hills High And Low: Walking The Herriot Way

A Walk On The Wild Side: The Yorkshire Wolds Way

Northbound On The West Highland Way

Hadrian's Wall Path: A Walk Through History

Rambling On: Lost On The Cleveland Way

Electric Dreams Road Trip

Printed in Great Britain
by Amazon